BEER

MAKES EVERYTHING BETTER

BEER

MAKES EVERYTHING BETTER

101 Recipes for Using Beer to Make Your Favorite Happy Hour Grub

JOHN LEMMON

Skyhorse Publishing

Skyhorse Publishing books may be purchased in bulk at special discounts for sales promotion, corporate gifts, fund-raising, or educational purposes. Special editions can also be created to specifications. For details, contact the Special Sales Department, Skyhorse Publishing, 307 West 36th Street, 11th Floor, New York, NY 10018 or info@skyhorsepublishing.com.

Skyhorse® and Skyhorse Publishing® are registered trademarks of Skyhorse Publishing, Inc.®, a Delaware corporation.

Visit our website at www.skyhorsepublishing.com.

10 9 8 7 6 5 4 3 2 1

Library of Congress Cataloging-in-Publication Data is available on file.

Cover design by Jane Sheppard
Jacket photographs: Shutterstock and iStockphoto

Print ISBN: 978-1-5107-0881-5
Ebook ISBN: 978-1-5107-0883-9

Printed in China

*To the love of my life, Jessica, who encouraged me
to follow my passion and write this book.*

Contents

INTRODUCTION

"I love to cook with beer, sometimes I even put it in my food."

Everyone loves Happy Hour . . . hey, that's why they call it "happy" . . . so why not create the same fun experience at home with great food and amazing beers? In this book you will learn how to make fifty fantastic recipes for your favorite grub, plus twenty awesome beer cocktails and ten beer shots sure to keep your party going long past closing time. And for the Sunday after, this book also features a quick-start beer brewing section with ten super simple ways to start brewing your own beer at home.

Beer Makes Everything Better is for the beer lover who wants to cook. It bridges the gap between two of the things you love most: eating and drinking. So what are you waiting for? Whether you're a reluctant short-order cook or a samurai sous chef, this book is like starting a party even if you only set a table for one.

Think beer is only for drinking? Think again. *Beer Makes Everything Better* is your answer to great food, great drinks, and most importantly—fun.

Why the heck should I buy this book?

Let's be honest, if you opened this book, you probably love beer, and, as a human, you need to eat. After a long day, drink specials and cheap apps at your local pub are nice, but what if you could enjoy great food and more in the comfort of your own home? Every beer lover should know how to infuse great beer flavor into your favorite foods, and you'll learn how to in this book. Whether entertaining friends or flying solo, this book will teach you how to create wonderful recipes and a personalized Happy Hour experience at home.

And, guess what? You're not limited to a few short hours on a weekday afternoon. No restrictions apply because Happy Hour starts and stops on your clock.

This cookbook is for the average, slightly lazy beer drinker who wants the down and dirty on great bar food without the fuss of poring over a stuffy manual. You will learn the quick and easy secrets to cooking and entertaining with beer, and even how to brew a batch of your own. After you see how easily you can make great bar food at home, I promise you will be hooked. And for those of you who want to have your beer and drink it too, look for my beer-belly-buster tips, which offer healthier options for your favorite appetizers.

Remember when I mentioned lazy? Good news. Even if the last book you read was in the third grade, you'll find plenty of pictures and tips to get you off to a quick start. Skimming is permitted. Whether you like lagers, pale ales, IPAs, or stouts, or you're looking for never-before-seen Happy Hour recipes, *Beer Makes Everything Better* will show you how to create great food and enjoy it with your favorite beers.

The party is waiting to happen. Just turn the page!

Why Happy Hour?

"My dad brewed beer and you couldn't imagine all the friends he had."
—My wife's grandpa, Gene Zink

I drank my first beer when I was in college, and to tell you the truth, I thought it tasted terrible. I was working at a restaurant and wanted to hang with the cool kids, so I knew I needed to like it. Back then, Happy Hour started after work and lasted until morning. Suffice to say, I got a lot of practice, and suddenly beer didn't taste so terrible any more.

After my restaurant job, I started bartending. I have always had a deep need in my soul to help someone relax after a long day by serving up the perfect beverage. Pairing drinks with delicious food is a win-win. I have spent a large portion of my life behind bars (ha) and even more time sitting at a bar (ha-ha), so what better way to share what I've learned than in this book?

Don't worry folks, I'm a professional.

Why did I start brewing?

My ridiculously intelligent older brother, David, was doing some research on our family history, and called to tell me about our great, great grandfather. Turned out Grampa Grimm was a brewer in our hometown of Springfield, Ohio, for thirty-two years. Legacy has always been important to me. Brewing beer was a legacy I could get behind!

By now I had developed a palate for craft beers, and what better way to carry on the family tradition than by perfecting what my grandfather had done for a living?

I headed out of the gates fast, brewing fifty batches in the first year alone. Since each batch was five gallons, we're talking two hundred and fifty gallons of beer. I couldn't drink it all myself, so you can imagine the friends I had.

I figured the more I brewed, the quicker I would learn. Since that life-changing year, I have hosted tasting parties, toured dozens of brewpubs, grown my own hops, and attended several brewing classes. I was even asked to partner with a local brewery to brew and sell my recipe at their taproom. With this rich history, personal experience, and family background, I couldn't resist sharing what I had learned.

CHAPTER 1

How to Use this Book—Permission to Spill Beer on the Pages, Use as a Coaster, and Dog-Ear the Corners

"He was a wise man, who invented beer."
—Plato

Let's face it, cooking food and mixing drinks can get messy. Don't freak out if you have a spill. Think of each splatter as marking your territory. This is your book and you get to put your own special signature on the pages.

If at any point you start getting frustrated with any process, do three things immediately:

1. Stop.
2. Take a deep breath.
3. Open a beer.

I understand that anything new can be challenging but if you follow those three steps, you will make it through okay.

Feel free to read this book in any order. Skip to the recipes if you want to get started. No, really, go to page 25, "Happy Hour at Home—Recipes and Pairings" and get your chef on. Browse the reference section if you need something specific. Read the end first if you like a good spoiler. Highlight words, sentences, or sections to make you feel all conversational.

If you didn't notice, the word "beer" is the biggest on the cover. That is because every recipe uses beer as an ingredient or the dish pairs nicely with the suggested brew. A few beer styles or brands might be difficult to find. Do your best and sub if necessary. If you feel adventurous you can experiment with different beers to see how the flavors turn out. Cooking with beer will add depth to your food and another layer of flavor. The more you cook with beer the more you will realize that beer does make everything better.

Most recipes will use only part of a beer. I suggest you drink the remainder to prevent waste and make the cooking process more enjoyable.

Each person has their own different palate. Taste each layer while you are cooking and add more seasoning or salt if necessary. The wings are a good example. I do not normally eat super hot wings. If you enjoy having your taste buds rocked and sweat pouring from your brow just double the cayenne pepper. Make notes in the margins so you can remember any tweaks or adjustments you customize.

This is your book; use it any way you like. I give you express written permission to do the following:

- Skim through if you find a section you're an expert on.
- Use as a coaster to protect your tabletop.
- Use the pictures as your recipe like when you refuse to read the directions for that shelf you are putting together. ("Hey, why do I have four screws left . . . ")
- Use as a flat surface to rest your beer on while at the beach.
- Use as a door stop while you bring in the groceries from the car.
- Hide it when you have friends over and pretend you just made up the coolest recipe.
- Use as a paperweight at the office to hold down your "TPS" reports.

- Read in the break room at work during lunch to make you look smarter.
- Read in the car while waiting to pick up your kids at school.
- Use as a weapon to bludgeon monsters during a zombie apocalypse.
- Balance on your head as you walk through the house to help your posture.
- Hand out to your favorite bartender to give them ideas.
- Break the spine so it stays open better.

I want you to make this book like that ten-year-old pair of your favorite jeans or like a security blanket when you were four. Comfortable and cozy.

My great-great-Grandpa Grimm, who inspired me to follow in his brewing footsteps.

CHAPTER 2

A Brief (Not Boring) History

*"She brews good ale, and thereof comes the proverb,
Blessing of your heart, you brew good ale."*
—William Shakespeare

*"In my opinion, most of the great men of the past were
only there for the beer . . ."*
—Alan John Percivale Taylor, British historian (1906–1990)

People have been making beer for over seven thousand years. Beer even has a cameo in the bible. If you think a brewery down the street has crafted the craziest honey ale, some Viking a thousand years ago was drinking a similar infusion. Vikings loved beer so much they would break mid battle to drink, and after filling up on liquid courage, rush back into battle shirtless and sometimes without armor. In Nordic, "berserk" means bare shirt, which is where the term "going berserk" comes from. Check out my Viking-inspired drink on page 114. Most of their beer was made from a combination of honey, grains, and herbs. This mead or ale was spoken of in songs, poems, and known as a drink of the gods. Legend has it Thor, the god of thunder, threw the coveted beer helmet to earth during a drunken rage. This sacred helmet held all the secrets to making great beer. Earthly Vikings then raided city after city in search of this magical helmet. Indiana Jones searching for the Holy Grail was child's play compared with Vikings on this quest.

During the early settlement of America, colonists brewed their own beer. My namesake, John Adams, the second president of the United States, wrote of his love of "Mr. Hairs" Porter to his wife Abigail. "It agrees with me, infinitely better than Punch, Wine, or Cider, or any other Spirituous Liquor." Sounds like President Adams liked beer as much as I do!

Brewing beer started out as a domestic or home project and only started being commercial after the Industrial Revolution. So by brewing your own beer at home like I teach in chapter 13, you are going back to your roots.

Over the years, styles and ingredients changed. One of the four main ingredients in beer, yeast, was not even known of until 1857 when it was discovered by Louis Pasteur. Following this discovery, brewers were able to understand the different strains of yeast and brew more consistently.

Two years before Lou's discovery, my great, great grandfather John (Johann) Grimm was born in Bern, Switzerland. In 1882 his family moved across the pond to the United States. The family settled in Springfield, Ohio. Four years after arriving in town, Grosspapa, as we called him, started working as a brewer at the Springfield Brewery. For the next thirty-two years of his life, the German and Swiss background came in handy when brewing traditional styles like lagers and pilsners. He worked until prohibition put the brewery out of business in 1918. Little did he know that he would inspire me to follow in his brewing footsteps almost a hundred years later.

Over time what was once a home or small munk operation turned into the huge commercial production it is today. Since the craft beer resurgence in the US in the 1980s, thousands of small craft breweries have opened across the country with towns such as Portland, Oregon, and Denver, Colorado, helping to lead the way. With the help of breweries such as Sam Adams Brewery and Dogfish Head Brewing, craft beer is now mainstream. My hometown of Dayton, Ohio, has gone from zero breweries to over fifteen in just five short years.

We can only guess at what the future of beer will be like. One thing is for sure—people will be enjoying it for years to come. Long live beer!

CHAPTER 3

EXPLORING
THE INGREDIENTS
AND FLAVORS

"Beer is proof that God loves us and wants us to be happy."
—Benjamin Franklin

There are four ingredients in beer. Water, barley, hops, and yeast. These four Horsemen of the Brew-pocalypse do all the work. Unlike the biblical horsemen, who bring destruction, these four friends combine to create every beer on earth. A tall order, but they love a challenge.

The Short Lesson Is:

Malted barley is steeped in warm water to release sugars. Think of it as a barley bath. Once the barley is removed, you are left with sugar-water called wort. Spelled with an "O" but pronounced wert with an "E." Silly English. The wort is then boiled for at least sixty minutes. During the boil, hops join the party to impart bitterness, flavor, and aroma. The wort is then cooled to room temperature and yeast is added, or "pitched." More like spilled. Yeast proceeds to eat the sugars in the wort and create alcohol. Once the yeast is finished chowing down, you are left with beer.

The last step is drinking! I am sure all this reading has made you thirsty. Why not head to the fridge and crack open a beer while you ponder this amazing process? Below is the shorter, more memorize-able version.

BEER MAKES EVERYTHING BETTER

The Super Short Lesson:

Barley + water = wort
Wort + hops = flavor
Yeast + wort = beer
Beer + you = ☺

The T-Shirt Version:

Barley + water + hops + yeast = beer = ☺

Flavors in Beer:

Beer has a bunch of flavor with only those four horsemen. To show off, brewers add other ingredients like fruit, herbs, and spices to impart even more taste. Cooking and pairing food with beer can release key flavors, creating a beautiful marriage. Like Westley and Buttercup, it may take some effort to get these kids together but when you do, magic happens. For example, lagers and pilsners pair nicely with Mexican food and light seafood dishes. Porters go well with smoked or BBQ foods like salmon, and spicy curry dishes work great with Indian Pale Ales (IPAs).

CHAPTER 4

ARE THERE HEALTH BENEFITS TO COOKING WITH BEER?

"Beer, if drunk in moderation, softens the temper, cheers the spirit, and promotes health."
—Thomas Jefferson

"A little bit of beer is divine medicine."
—Paracelsus, Greek physician

I know it seems crazy, but enjoying craft beer may have some health benefits. Don't get me wrong—sitting on the couch and slamming a dozen gas station light beers and chowing double meat pizzas every night won't help you live longer. But studies have shown ingredients like soluble fiber, B vitamins, antioxidants, and silicon, all found in beer, may have health benefits. Other research shows craft beer has more health benefits than red wine. By subbing beer for heavy cream, eggs, or other fatty ingredients, you could help lower the calorie and fat content of the food you cook and add great flavors in the process. Before you go running to your favorite local brewpub to fill your prescription during Happy Hour, let's explore four possible benefits of craft beer.

Beer is rich in B vitamins

Beer contains B vitamins from the ingredient yeast. Unfiltered beer, like homebrew, contains considerable amounts of B3 and B6. According to Jennifer J. Brown, PhD, in an article on www.everydayhealth.com, "B vitamins help promote a healthy metabolism and are also linked to a reduced risk of stroke, research shows."

Beer contains fiber

Fiber has many health benefits. Most famously, it helps with digestion. Darker beers have a higher concentration of fiber. Fiber is found in most fruits. Fruit juices contain more sugar than beer. So if you drink a dark beer with your breakfast, you will have similar benefits, but with less sugar than orange juice. Something to consider for your next Sunday brunch.

Beer contains silicon

Beer could help prevent Alzheimer's disease? Possibly, according to a study at a university in Spain. Their research concludes "moderate beer consumption, possibly affording a protective factor for the toxic effect of aluminum, one of the environmental factors for Alzheimer's disease." I'll drink to that!

Reduced chances of heart attack or stroke

A beer a day keeps the doctor away? I wouldn't go that far, but according to the Mayo Clinic, alcohol may reduce the risk of dying from a heart attack and possibly reduces the risk of stroke. Of course, this is regarding "moderate" beer drinking, which is defined as twelve ounces per day for women and twenty-four ounces per day for men.

CHAPTER 5

SHOPPING FOR THE BEST INGREDIENTS

"You don't have to cook fancy or complicated masterpieces—just good food from fresh ingredients."
—Julia Child

No matter what you are making, the fresher the ingredients, the better. Cooking up your own Happy Hour (or brewing beer) is no different. Even if you don't have a super picky palate, non-fresh ingredients will be easy to notice. When purchasing ingredients for a recipe, do your best to buy what is local and freshest. Plan your cooking close to the day you hit the grocery. That way you don't end up wasting food that sits too long in the bottom fridge drawer. My wife refers to that as the "rotter" because if you don't use the food quickly it could end up resembling a science experiment.

Seasonality is also important. As an example: apples and pumpkins are freshest in the fall just like most berries are best in the spring and summer. Local farmers' markets are a great place to get fresh, seasonal food. Fruits, vegetables, eggs, meat, and even flowers can be found at these markets.

When brewing beer, the same rules apply. Older hops will impart less flavor, older yeast is less likely to ferment correctly, and old barley could cause an off taste. Like drinking out of an old shoe. Always check the dates when purchasing ingredients from your local homebrew store. If buying online it helps to email the site to confirm the item they are sending is fresh.

Fresh herbs are an easy way to add tons of flavor to your food. You can grow most herbs in a garden or even grow inside during the winter months using a sunny window. I have grown basil, thyme, mint, and parsley. Nothing is fresher than picking herbs straight off the plant and adding to your dish. If you don't have a green thumb, most groceries have fresh herbs you can use.

CHAPTER 6

SUPPLIES AND QUICK START GUIDE TO BREWING YOUR OWN

"From man's sweat and God's love, beer came into the world."
—Saint Arnold of Metz, The Patron Saint of Brewers

This chapter is important even if you do not plan on brewing. If you at least skim the chapter and scan the pictures, you will learn enough to comprehend the brewing process. This will help answer your friend's questions, appreciate a brewery tour, or even answer random trivia questions at your local pub—from mash tun, to hot liquor tank, to boil kettle, to fermenter, to bright tank. You will understand what equipment is used for each step and what you will need to brew your first batch. I will take you step by step through the brewing process used at a commercial brewery and then show you how to brew at home on a smaller scale. The process is the same, except the equipment is reduced and you won't need a full staff to crank out your first batch.

Like we discussed in chapter 3, there are four main ingredients in beer: barley, hops, water, and yeast. Brewers start with malted barley or other cereal grains. Soaking this in warm water will extract the sugars in the grains. Using a mash tun filled with warm water, normally around 150°F they stir in the grains. Most beer recipes let the grains soak (or rest) for at least an hour. When you brew your beer at home with my recipes, we will be using liquid malt extract to make the process easier. Liquid malt extract, or LME, is concentrated sugar from grains.

After the sugar has been extracted from the grains, brewers move the sugary water, known as wort, to the boil kettle. The wort is then boiled for sixty to ninety minutes and hops are added at specific times to impart different flavors. Hops added at the beginning of the boil are added for bitterness. They will offset the sweetness of the sugary wort. Hops added during the middle of the boil will impart flavor, and hops added at the end will impart aroma. Brewers even add hops after the boil to add extra aroma—this process is called "dry hopping." If you have ever had a super aromatic IPA, you will know that it was dry hopped.

Once the boil is completed, the wort needs to be chilled to around 70°F. You can use a wort chiller for this process or just simply place your boil kettle in an ice bath and stir until cool.

After the wort is chilled, it is transferred to a fermenting vessel. Large breweries use huge stainless steel tanks for this. But we are just using a glass carboy or a

fermenting bucket. Once the wort is transferred to the fermenter, the yeast is pitched. Yeast can be dry or liquid form. The yeast will start to eat the sugars in the wort and turn it to alcohol. The amount of sugar the yeast is able to consume will determine the alcohol content of the final beer. You can see this amount on most bottles of beer indicated as the ABV, or Alcohol by Volume. Most lagers or ales are around 5 percent, while stronger beers like double IPAs or imperial stouts can be over 10 percent.

Fermentation normally lasts two to four weeks. Once this is complete and the yeast has eaten all the sugars, you are left with beer. There is only one more step: Carbonation. Breweries use a bright tank to add CO_2 gas to the beer, and then keg or bottle it for sale. Homebrewers use a different method to carbonate their beer. By adding a small measured amount of sugar to the beer right before bottling, the leftover yeast will chow down on this small amount of sugar and in turn give the beer some life. The coolest thing about home brewing is opening your beer and hearing the fizz noise confirming you just made beer! Nothing is better.

One other method of carbonation used by sophisticated homebrewers is kegging beer in five gallon corny kegs and adding CO_2 gas to force carbonate the brew. You will need more gear and an empty fridge to store the kegs. But being able to pour a smooth draft of your own brew can be very rewarding.

Now that you have an overview, I will give you specific instructions on what you need and how to use this gear to make your first one-gallon batch at home.

The equipment and ingredients need to brew an easy one-gallon batch can be found at your local homebrew store and directions are on the following page. If you do not have a store close by you can order everything you need online. Go to www.thathappyhourguy.com/supplies for personal recommendations of the best places to purchase everything from equipment to ingredients.

Equipment

Large pot (8-quart size or larger. A large soup pot will work great.)

1.5 gallon fermenting bucket with airlock

Auto-siphon and tubing

Bottle filler and capper

12 beer bottles and caps

Sanitizer

Hydrometer to measure the gravity (optional)

You will also need the beer ingredients. Below are the ingredients for my own David's First IPA 1-gallon recipe.

1.5 gallons water (spring or good tasting tap water)

2 pounds of Muntons 2-row malted barley

0.25 pounds of Crisp Crystal 15L malted barley

Grain bag

1.5 pounds of regular Liquid Malt Extract

1-ounce package of Amarillo Hop Pellets

Yeast: Safale US-05 dry yeast (half packet)

1 ounce of corn sugar (for priming)

Brewing Directions:

1. In a large pot, on high heat, start heating the 1.5 gallons of water. Place the crushed malts in a grain bag and tie off the end. Once the water reaches 155°F, turn off the heat and add the grain bag. "Mash" the grain bag for 20 minutes at 150–155°F, stirring occasionally. After 20 minutes, remove the grain bag and hold above the pot to let it drain (do not squeeze the bag). The colored water is now called wort.

2. Turn heat back on and bring to a boil. Once boiling, remove from heat and slowly mix in the Liquid Malt Extract (LME). Put back on the heat and return to a boil once the LME is thoroughly mixed in.

3. Divide the Amarillo Hop Pellets into four equal parts. Start a 60-minute timer and stir in ¼ of the bittering hops Amarillo Pellets. After 30 minutes, add another ¼ of the flavoring hops. After 15 minutes, add the next ¼ of the pellets. In 15 more minutes, turn off heat and add the final ¼ Amarillo Pellets for aroma. Stir wort for a few minutes.

4. Fill a sink with cold water and ice, then put the covered kettle in the ice bath. The goal is to cool the wort to approximately 70–72°F when the kettle is cool to the touch. The yeast is happiest at these temperatures.

5. Use sanitized hydrometer to measure the O.G. (original gravity).

6. Transfer cooled wort to sanitized fermenting container. Close lid and aerate (slosh back and forth) for 1 minute. Yeast cells need some oxygen for a healthy fermentation.

7. Open fermenter and, using sanitized yeast packet and scissors, pour half the packet into the wort. Close lid and install air lock (fill halfway with sanitizer or water).

8. Move fermenter to a cool dark area with an ideal temperature between 65°F and 72°F.

9. To celebrate, open your fridge and pour yourself a well-deserved beer!

After fermentation is complete in 14–21 days, your beer will be ready to bottle.

Bottling Directions:

1. Clean and sanitize: the large pot you used for cooking the beer, the auto-siphon, tubing, bottle filler, and 12 bottles and caps.

2. In a small pot, combine 1 cup of water and 1 ounce of corn sugar. Heat and boil for 5 minutes. Let cool and add to large pot.

3. Open the fermenter. Use the auto-siphon and tubing to transfer the beer into the large pot. Stir slowly to combine the sugar water.

4. Use the auto-siphon and bottle filler to start filling the beer bottles. Make sure you don't overfill the bottles, leaving an inch or so of space at the top of each.

5. Use the capper to cap all the bottles. Place them in a dark area at room temperature.

6. Congratulations! You have just brewed and bottled your first beer. It normally takes 2 more weeks for your beer to be ready to drink. But feel free to wait longer. Your beer will only get better with age.

7. Chill your beer and open and pour into a pint glass. Stare at it for a few minutes and enjoy!

So there you have it—everything you need to brew your first batch of beer at home. Please visit www.thathappyhourguy.com for videos and articles about brewing and beer.

CHAPTER 7

HAPPY HOUR AT HOME—RECIPES AND PAIRINGS

"I work until beer o'clock."
—Stephen King

If you ask my wife, she'll say cooking isn't my strong suit—but I've done my share in the kitchen. And I don't mean just washing dishes. My experience includes working with chefs at three different restaurants. I have drawn from this experience and taken the guesswork out of preparing Happy Hour food at home.

The first section will show you how to cook using your favorite beers. I put a new twist on old favorites, like beer cheese soup, and invented a few you have never heard of. Boozy Brussels sprouts anyone? Adding beer to food will get your Happy Hour started!

The next section pairs my favorite dishes with beer. It is surprising how beer can cause hidden flavors to stand out.

The last section is for the morning after. These meals will get you back to the "land of the living" after a rough night.

Even if you're new to the kitchen and your go-to meal is microwaved hot dogs, the directions are easy to follow. You don't have to be a sous chef in a fancy restaurant to understand.

The recipes are carefully tested to ensure each dish turns out well. Beginners will find it easy to jump right in with confidence.

Savoring the Savory

"Beer is good food."
—John Goodman

Beer Cheese Fondue

Serves 2–4

I like to use a light flavored beer to add to, but not overpower, the strong Gouda and cheddar. Beer and cheese: need I say more?

Ingredients:

¾ cup beer
1 garlic clove, minced
½ cup Swiss cheese,
    shredded
½ cup Gouda, shredded
½ cup sharp cheddar cheese,
    shredded
1 tablespoon cornstarch
1 teaspoon Frank's hot sauce
1 teaspoon Worcestershire
    sauce

Directions:

1. Heat beer in large pot slowly over medium to low heat.

2. Add garlic.

3. Toss shredded cheese with cornstarch. Once beer is warm, slowly add cheese.

4. Lower heat and stir constantly with a whisk until all cheese is melted, 5–10 minutes.

5. Once beer and cheese are nicely melded together, stir in hot sauce and Worcestershire. Use beer to thin out if too thick.

6. Dip cubed French bread or bagels in fondue.

PRO TIP

Heat is the key! If it is too hot, the cheese will break. Too cool and the cheese will not melt or it will set up. Watch the heat closely.

IPA BBQ Sauce

This tangy, sweet, homemade BBQ sauce will make you wonder why you ever tried store-bought sauces.

Ingredients:

1 tablespoon olive oil
½ cup white onion, thinly diced
1 garlic clove, minced
2 cups ketchup
1 tablespoon yellow mustard
½ cup brown sugar
1 tablespoon honey
1 tablespoon Worcestershire
  sauce
2 tablespoons apple cider
  vinegar
1 tablespoon molasses
1 teaspoon black pepper
6 ounces of your favorite IPA
  (the stronger the better)

Directions:

1. Heat olive oil in medium pot over medium-high heat.

2. Add onion and garlic. Sauté for 2–3 minutes or until onion is clear.

3. Add remaining ingredients to pot.

4. Simmer over medium-low heat, stirring occasionally for 10–15 minutes or until sauce is nice and thick.

5. Let cool completely.

PRO TIP

Make ahead and store in a Mason jar overnight for a richer flavor.

Crabby Dip

Makes enough dip for 4–6

Get over your case of the Mondays with this fancy fake out!

Ingredients:

1 (8-ounce) package cream
    cheese, softened
1 garlic clove, minced
½ cup lager beer
⅔ cup sour cream
⅓ tablespoon mayo
1 cup mozzarella cheese,
    shredded
1 cup cheddar, shredded
1 teaspoon salt
1 teaspoon Old Bay
    seasoning
Dash of cayenne pepper, or
    to taste
12 ounces imitation crab,
    chopped into chunks
½ cup green onions, halved
    and chopped
Crackers or bagel chips

Directions:

1. Preheat oven to 375°F.

2. Soften cream cheese by leaving at room temperature or microwave for 1 minute.

3. In a large bowl, combine garlic, cream cheese, beer, sour cream, mayo, mozzarella, ½ cup cheddar, salt, Old Bay, and cayenne.

4. Carefully stir in imitation crab and ¼ cup green onions.

5. Transfer to oven-safe loaf pan and bake for 25–30 minutes or until hot in the middle.

6. Top with remaining ½ cup cheddar and bake for 5 more minutes.

7. Remove from oven and garnish with remaining ¼ cup green onions.

8. Serve with crackers or bagel chips.

Beer Sautéed Shrimp and Scallops

Makes 2 servings

I can never decide which I love better, shrimp or scallops. With this dish you don't have to choose.

Ingredients:

½ pound raw shrimp, peeled and deveined
½ pound large bay scallops
2 tablespoons butter
2 cloves of garlic, minced
½ cup light beer
2 tablespoons lemon juice
Salt and pepper
¼ cup fresh basil, torn into small pieces

Directions:

1. Pat dry shrimp and scallops and season with salt and pepper.

2. In a large pan, sauté the garlic in butter for one minute.

3. Add shrimp and scallops to pan and cook 2–3 minutes per side, or until browned.

4. Add beer, lemon juice, salt, and pepper. Bring to a boil, then simmer for 3–4 minutes. Liquid should reduce to about half.

5. Stir in basil.

6. Remove shrimp and scallops first and pour sauce over top.

7. Serve in small bowls.

PRO TIP

You can tell when the shrimp are done cooking when they turn pink and curl up like the letter "C."

Batter Up: Homemade Beer Battered Fish

Makes 2 servings

If you have never had beer battered fish, you are in for a treat.

Ingredients:

1 cup flour
1 tablespoon baking powder
1 teaspoon salt
¼ teaspoon black pepper
¼ teaspoon cayenne pepper
2 teaspoon Old Bay
    seasoning
1 beer (Gold Pants Pale Ale
    or your favorite ale)
4 pieces of white fish
    (something firm like
    tilapia, cod, etc.)
2–4 tablespoons cornstarch

Directions:

1. In a bowl, whisk together the flour, baking powder, salt, black pepper, cayenne pepper, and Old Bay seasoning.

2. Whisk in beer until the batter is completely smooth and free of any lumps. Refrigerate for at least 15 minutes.

3. Dredge each piece of fish in cornstarch, then dip in batter.

4. Heat 2–4 inches of vegetable oil in a large pot. When oil reaches 365°F, fry fish, turning every 2–3 minutes until done.

5. Remove from oil and place on plate with paper towels to drain the oil. Salt immediately after placing on plate.

6. Serve with tartar sauce and a lemon wedge.

PRO TIP

Use one hand to dredge the fish in cornstarch and drop in the batter. Use the other hand to remove from the batter. This makes it easier to keep the cornstarch dry.

BEER MAKES EVERYTHING BETTER

Tartar Sauce

Prepare this to serve with the Beer Battered Fish!

Ingredients:

¼ cup mayo
1 tablespoon dill pickle
  relish
1 teaspoon mustard
⅛ teaspoon hot sauce
⅛ teaspoon lemon juice
Salt and pepper

Directions:

1. Combine all ingredients in small bowl.

Tinfoil Tater Tots with IPA BBQ Sauce

Makes a snack or side dish for 4–6

This is the perfect side to complement anything you put on the grill. The tinfoil cooking method makes it easy to cook up the tots along with your favorite grill grub. Pair with IPA BBQ Sauce on page 29!

Ingredients:

1 bag of tots
Salt and pepper

Directions:

1. Spray a large sheet of aluminum foil with nonstick cooking spray.

2. Add tots to one side of the foil. Sprinkle with salt and pepper to taste.

3. Fold over other half and crimp edges to seal.

4. Cook on grill at medium heat for 7–8 minutes per side or until golden brown.

Beer Batter

Ingredients:

½ cup flour
½ tablespoon baking powder
½ teaspoon salt
¼ teaspoon black pepper
¼ teaspoon cayenne pepper
1 teaspoon taco seasoning
½ bottle dark Mexican beer

Directions:

1. In a bowl, whisk together the flour, baking powder, salt, black pepper, cayenne pepper, and taco seasoning.

2. Whisk in the beer until the batter is completely smooth and free of any lumps. Refrigerate for at least 15 minutes.

Cerveza-Battered Halibut Wrap

Makes 2 wraps

Using a dark Mexican beer in the batter gives the halibut a great flavor.

Ingredients:

½ pound of halibut, sliced
    into 1-inch strips
2 tablespoons cornstarch
Beer Batter (recipe above)
Vegetable or canola oil for
    frying
Medium-sized burrito wrap
½ cup shredded lettuce
½ tomato, diced
½ avocado, sliced
1 tablespoon sour cream
Salsa, to taste
1 tablespoon fresh cilantro

Directions:

1. Pat dry fish with a paper towel. Dredge in cornstarch, then dip in batter.

2. Heat 2–4 inches of vegetable or canola oil in a medium pot. When oil reaches 365°F, fry fish, turning every 3–4 minutes until done.

3. Remove from oil and place on plate with paper towels to drain the oil.

4. Add lettuce, tomato, avocado, sour cream, salsa, and halibut to burrito wrap.

5. Top with cilantro. Roll or fold together and enjoy!

Tailgate Turkey Chili

Makes 4–6 servings

This hearty chili is perfect for game day. Double the recipe if you plan on a bigger crowd.

Ingredients:

1 tablespoon olive oil
½ white onion, diced
2 garlic cloves, minced
1 red pepper, diced
1 pound ground turkey
1 teaspoon salt
½ teaspoon black pepper
1 teaspoon chili powder
¼ teaspoon cayenne pepper
   (¼ is mild—add ½ or
   more to kick the heat up!)
1 can of white beans (rinse
   before using)
1 (14.5-ounce) can of
   crushed tomatoes
1 cup beer (the Jessica Red
   works great or your
   favorite medium beer)
2 cups of water
1 teaspoon cornstarch

Directions:

1. Add olive oil to large pot. Over medium-high heat, cook onion, garlic, and red pepper until the onion is clear, 3–5 minutes.

2. Add 1 pound of ground turkey, using a wooden spoon to break turkey into small pieces as it browns.

3. Stir in salt, pepper, chili powder, and cayenne pepper.

4. Once turkey is fully cooked, add beans, crushed tomatoes, beer, and water. Simmer over low heat for 45 minutes.

5. Combine 1 teaspoon cornstarch with 3 teaspoons water. Stir until there are no lumps. Add to chili, stirring slowly for 5 minutes.

6. Salt and pepper to taste, and serve!

PRO TIP

Garnish with cilantro, sour cream, cheese, or any other tasty item you have in the fridge.

Po Boy Sandwiches

Makes 2 sandwiches

Not many things are better than fried shrimp. This recipe puts the delicious shrimp on a sandwich.

Ingredients:

6–8 raw jumbo shrimp, fried using the beer batter recipe on page 32. Use 3–4 per sandwich.
2 hoagie buns (uncut work best)
Lettuce, shredded
Tomato, sliced
Mayo (or remoulade sauce, see below)

Remoulade sauce:
½ cup mayonnaise
1 tablespoon stone ground mustard
1 teaspoon water
1 teaspoon prepared horseradish
1 teaspoon white onion, minced
1 teaspoon green bell pepper, minced
½ teaspoon fresh parsley, minced
½ teaspoon white vinegar
¼ teaspoon paprika
¼ teaspoon ground black pepper
¼ teaspoon ground cayenne pepper
1 pinch salt
½ teaspoon fresh lemon juice

Sandwich Directions:

1. Follow the Beer Batter directions on page 32 to prepare the batter.

2. Heat 2–4 inches of vegetable or canola oil in a medium pot. When oil reaches 365°F, fry shrimp, turning every 2–3 minutes until done.

3. Slice hoagies three quarters of the way in half.

4. Put lettuce, tomato, shrimp, and mayo (or remoulade) together to form sandwich. I suggest using the awesome remoulade sauce recipe provided here!

Remoulade Sauce Directions:

1. Mix all ingredients together in small bowl.

Beer Baked Wings

Serves 6–8

Plan ahead and marinate overnight for best results.

Ingredients:

2 pounds of wings
1 beer of choice
2 tablespoons olive oil
2 garlic cloves, chopped
1 tablespoon dry mustard
2 teaspoons ground cumin
½ teaspoon cayenne
   pepper (for a much
   hotter version, use 1½
   tablespoons)
1 teaspoon freshly cracked
   black pepper
1 teaspoon kosher salt
1 teaspoon brown sugar

Directions:

1. Rinse wings and let dry.

2. Whisk together the rest of the ingredients. Marinate wings in container or ziplock bag overnight in fridge.

3. The next day, preheat oven to 375°F.

4. Use rack on top of edged baking sheet covered with foil (for easy cleanup).

5. Spray rack with nonstick cooking spray. Remove wings from marinade and place wings skin side up and cook for 45–55 minutes.

6. Brush on small amount of marinade after 20 minutes. (Optional)

PRO TIP

Save ¼ of the dry seasoning and sprinkle on the wings before putting in the oven. This will add more flavor.

Beer Broth Mussels

Serves 2

A light beer will give the mussels a fresh taste.

Ingredients:

2 pounds of mussels
1 tablespoon olive oil
1 garlic clove, minced
1 beer (something light)
Salt and pepper to taste
A pinch of cayenne pepper
1 tablespoon butter
1 tablespoon sugar
1 teaspoon Dijon or hot
mustard
1 teaspoon parsley, chopped

Directions:

1. Rinse mussels in cold water.

2. In large pot (make sure you have a lid), sauté the garlic in 1 tablespoon olive oil for one minute.

3. Add beer, salt, pepper, and cayenne. Stir until beer starts to boil.

4. Reduce heat, add mussels, and cover. Cook covered for 7–10 minutes or until most of the mussels have opened.

5. Use slotted spoon to remove mussels and discard any unopened ones.

6. Place in flat bowl.

7. Add butter, sugar, mustard, and parsley to pot. Bring to boil and whisk until smooth.

8. Remove from heat and pour small amount over mussels.

9. Enjoy!

PRO TIP

Dip beer bread from page 53 in sauce for a more hearty meal.

Irish Glazed Salmon

Serves 1

According to my brother, the ancestry guru, I am ⅛ᵗʰ Irish. I am also a big fan of Irish bands and Irish stouts. Watching an Irish band perform on St. Patty's Day while enjoying a pint is a yearly tradition.

This glazed salmon recipe works best with a nice mild stout like the ⅛th Irish Stout on page 135 but could also be tasty using an amber ale like Amber's Easy Ale on page 118. The sweet glaze has a nice smoky flavor. If you are sick of BBQ chicken or need some omega 3's in your diet, this is the perfect dish for you!

Ingredients:

1 tablespoon olive oil
1 medium shallot (or red
   onion if you prefer)
⅓ cup Irish stout (or amber
   ale for a lighter glaze)
1 tablespoon soy sauce
2 tablespoons molasses
½ tablespoon brown sugar
¼ teaspoon liquid smoke
¼ teaspoon smoked paprika
¼ teaspoon cumin
¼ teaspoon black pepper,
   ground
1 piece of salmon, 8–10
   ounces

Directions:

1. Preheat oven broiler to 450°F.

2. In medium pot, sauté shallots in olive oil over medium-high heat, 2–3 minutes or until softened and lightly browned.

3. Add beer, soy sauce, molasses, brown sugar, liquid smoke, paprika, cumin, and black pepper. Stir together and bring to a boil.

4. Reduce heat to medium, stirring occasionally until it starts to thicken, about 5–10 minutes. Be careful not to let the sugar burn to the bottom of the pot.

5. Line an edged baking sheet with aluminum foil. Apply a small amount of oil or cooking spray to the foil.

Continued on page 40.

6. Cut the salmon into 2-inch filets. Place thawed salmon on the foil, skin side down, and lightly salt.

7. Broil for 5 minutes. Remove and use brush (or spoon) to apply glaze to the top of the salmon. Use as much as you can without getting too much on the foil because it will burn.

8. Broil for 2–3 minutes at a time, adding more glaze in between. Total cook time should be 10–15 minutes or until light and flaky.

9. Serve with small amount of glaze on top.

Super Foodie Quinoa Salad & Raspberry Lambic Vinaigrette

Serves 2

This healthy but tasty salad is a great summer treat.

Ingredients:

Raspberry Vinaigrette:
½ cup raspberries
¼ cup olive oil
2 tablespoons fresh lemon juice
2 tablespoons honey
¼ cup lambic beer
Salt and pepper to taste

Salad:
1 cup quinoa
1 large bunch of kale
½ avocado, diced (optional)
¼ cup blue cheese or feta
½ cup dried cranberries
¼ cup sliced almonds
Salt and pepper, to taste

Vinaigrette Directions:

1. Combine all ingredients *except* beer in blender.

2. Once blended, stir in beer with whisk.

3. Add salt and pepper to taste.

Salad Directions:

1. Cook quinoa according to directions on box and let cool. Make sure you rinse the quinoa before cooking. You could make this ahead of time or even the day before and store it in the fridge.

2. Remove stems from the kale and chop into small pieces.

3. Break up cheese into small pieces.

4. Combine all ingredients and mix in the dressing.

5. Taste and add salt and pepper if needed.

Boozy Brussels Sprouts

Serves 2–4

Your mother always told you to eat your veggies. This recipe will make your taste buds and mother happy.

Ingredients:

2 tablespoons olive oil

½ cup shallots, sliced

1 garlic clove, minced

1 pound Brussels sprouts, halved

1 light flavorful beer of choice (the Honey Wheat Ale on page 124 will work nicely)

½ teaspoon salt

¼ teaspoon black pepper

¼ teaspoon crushed red pepper flakes

1 teaspoon liquid smoke

Directions:

1. Sauté the garlic and shallots in olive oil for 2–3 minutes.

2. Add sprouts and cook for 4–5 minutes or until the sides of the sprouts are lightly brown.

3. Add beer, salt, pepper, red pepper, and liquid smoke.

4. Reduce heat and simmer for around 15 minutes or until the beer has reduced to a glaze.

5. Serve as appetizer. Also makes a great side dish for a larger meal.

Kickass Shroom Burger

Makes 5 medium burgers

These non-meat burgers really are kickass. The IPA BBQ sauce gives it a great smoky flavor.

Ingredients:

1 tablespoon olive oil
10 ounces baby portobello mushrooms, chopped very fine in a food processor or with a knife
1 shallot, thinly sliced
½ teaspoon salt
1 teaspoon thyme
¼ teaspoon black pepper
1 (15-ounce) can of kidney beans
2 tablespoons IPA BBQ sauce (page 29)
1 teaspoon smoked paprika
½ teaspoon onion powder
½ teaspoon garlic powder
½ cup flour
Burger buns

Directions:

1. Preheat oven to 400°F.

2. Heat olive oil in a pan over medium-high heat. Cook mushrooms and shallots until mushrooms release their water and begin to brown. Add salt, thyme, and pepper.

3. Drain and rinse kidney beans. In a large bowl, mash with fork until there are no whole beans left.

4. Mix in mushrooms, shallots, barbecue sauce, paprika, onion powder, garlic powder, and flour. Add extra barbecue sauce or a splash of water if the mixture is too dry.

5. Line baking sheet with parchment paper and spray with cooking spray.

6. Divide mixture into fifths and form into patties.

7. Bake 10 minutes on each side, or until burgers are solid and cooked throughout.

8. Serve on burger buns and garnish with burger toppings!

Turkey Beer Sliders

Makes 8 sliders

For a more traditional taste sub the turkey with ground sirloin.

Ingredients:

1 pound of ground
turkey (93/7 is a good
percentage of fat)
1 teaspoon olive oil
¼ beer (something strong
like David's First IPA on
page 116)
½ onion or 1 medium
shallot, finely chopped
½ bell pepper, finely
chopped (use your
favorite color)
1 tablespoon fresh parsley,
chopped
1 tablespoon hot sauce
½ teaspoon salt
¼ teaspoon black pepper
⅛ teaspoon cayenne pepper
8 small slices of pepper jack
cheese
1 package of slider buns

Directions:

1. Over medium heat, sauté onion and bell pepper in olive oil and beer for 5–6 minutes or until softened.

2. Except the last two ingredients, mix everything together in a medium bowl. Form into eight patties.

3. Cook patties over medium heat in pan on stove with small amount of olive or butter. Cook 4–5 minutes per side.

4. Add cheese after final flip to melt.

5. Serve on slider buns with ketchup, mayo, pickle, lettuce, or other such burger fixins.

Spin Dip!

Serves 4–6

This Happy Hour classic gets a reboot by adding a light-colored beer, but feel free to use a strong IPA for an exciting twist.

Ingredients:

1 tablespoon olive oil
½ medium white onion, minced
2 garlic cloves, minced
1 (12-ounce) package frozen
    chopped spinach
1 (14-ounce) can artichoke hearts,
    drained and coarsely chopped
¼ cup beer (something light
    like the Cascading Centennial
    Blonde on page 122)
2 (8-ounce) packages cream
    cheese, softened
2 tablespoons sour cream
1 cup mozzarella cheese, shredded
½ cup Parmesan, shredded
1 teaspoon salt
½ teaspoon crushed red pepper
¼ teaspoon black pepper
¼ teaspoon dried basil
Dash of cayenne pepper, or more
    to taste
Veggies, pita chips, or tortilla
    chips

Directions:

1. Preheat oven to 400°F.

2. Heat olive oil in large pan over medium heat. Cook onions 3–4 minutes or until onions are clear. Add garlic with 1 minute left.

3. Stir in spinach, artichokes, and beer until warm throughout.

4. Add cream cheese, sour cream, mozzarella, Parmesan, salt, red pepper, black pepper, basil, and cayenne and stir until smooth.

5. Transfer to an oven-safe dish (a 9-inch pie pan works well) and bake for 20 minutes or until the top is toasty.

6. Serve with veggies, pita chips, or tortilla chips.

Nacho Beer Cheese Dip

Serves 4–6

I like to use a light American lager for a subtle beer flavor. Put this dip in a crock-pot for easy transportation to your next party.

Ingredients:

1 tablespoon olive oil
2 garlic cloves, minced
½ cup beer
1 teaspoon ground cumin
½ teaspoon dried oregano
1 (16-ounce) can black beans
1 cup chunky salsa (medium or hot)
¼ cup hot sauce
1 (16-ounce) package Velveeta cheese
¼ cup chopped fresh cilantro
Tortilla chips

Directions:

1. In a large pan, sauté the garlic in 1 tablespoon olive oil for one minute.

2. Add beer, cumin, and dried oregano. Bring to simmer.

3. Add beans, salsa, and hot sauce, stirring until heated. Reduce heat to medium low.

4. Cut Velveeta into ½-inch cubes and add to pot. Stir in a handful at a time until all are melted.

5. Stir in cilantro.

6. Transfer to bowl or slow cooker. Chow down with chips!

PRO TIP

This dip goes great as a topping for baked potatoes.

Lager Roasted Turkey Gyro with "T" Sauce

Serves 2

Ingredients:

1 tablespoon olive oil
1 garlic clove, minced
½ cup beer (a nice lager works great)
½ teaspoon oregano
½ teaspoon rosemary
½ pound turkey, sliced medium thick
2 pitas or flat bread slices
Cucumber slices
Tomato, diced
Lettuce
Fresh baby spinach

"T" sauce:
½ cup Greek yogurt
¼ teaspoon garlic salt
½ teaspoon lemon zest
¼ teaspoon fresh dill and/or fresh mint
Salt & pepper to taste

Gyro Directions:

1. In a large pan, sauté the garlic in 1 tablespoon olive oil for one minute.

2. Add beer, oregano, and rosemary and simmer on low for 5 minutes.

3. Add turkey and slow cook for 5 minutes or until the turkey has browned lightly. Turn halfway through.

4. Remove turkey from pan. Build gyro by putting turkey on flatbread or in pita pocket.

5. Add cucumber, tomato, lettuce, spinach, and "T" sauce.

Sauce Directions:

1. In small bowl, combine yogurt, garlic salt, lemon zest, dill (or mint) and salt & pepper. Stir until smooth.

Chili Cheese Tots

Serves 2–4

Kick your tots up to the next level by adding the beer-infused Tailgate Turkey Chili leftover from your last game day.

Ingredients:

1 bag of frozen potato "tots"
Salt and pepper
Shredded cheddar cheese
Tailgate Turkey Chili
  (page 35)

Directions:

1. Cook tots using directions on package.

2. Once fully cooked, remove from oven and stack in soup bowl. Salt and pepper to taste.

3. Top with chili and shredded cheese and enjoy!

Mustard Pale Ale Sauce

Ingredients:

1 tablespoon olive oil
1 garlic clove, minced
½ cup pale ale (a moderately hoppy beer works best)
¼ cup spicy brown mustard
¼ cup yellow mustard
1 tablespoon pickle relish
2 teaspoons agave nectar
1 teaspoon horseradish
½ teaspoon hot sauce
¼ teaspoon lemon juice
⅛ teaspoon salt
⅛ teaspoon ground black pepper

Directions:

1. Sauté garlic in olive oil over medium heat in medium pan for 2–3 minutes.

2. Add beer, reduce heat, and simmer until beer is reduced to about half, about 5–6 minutes.

3. Stir in remaining ingredients and remove from heat.

4. Serve warm or chill in fridge overnight.

Pasta with White Ale Cream Sauce

Serves 2

Breaking tradition and using beer instead of wine gives the sauce a creamier finish. Using a nitro-infused pub ale would work even better.

Ingredients:

8 ounces elbow pasta (half a box)
2 tablespoons olive oil
2 cloves garlic, minced
1 cup white ale (any light wheat beer will work)
½ cup light cream (or substitute)
½ teaspoon fresh rosemary, minced
¼ teaspoon red pepper flakes
Salt and black pepper to taste
1 tablespoon butter
8 ounces mushrooms, cubed
1 zucchini, small cubes
Parmesan cheese

Directions:

1. Cook pasta al dente according to package.

2. In a large pan, sauté the garlic in 1 tablespoon olive oil for one minute.

3. Add ale, cream, rosemary, red pepper, salt and pepper. Simmer for 5–10 min or until sauce starts to thicken.

4. Add butter and stir for additional 1–2 minutes.

5. In a separate pan, sauté mushrooms and zucchini using 1 tablespoon olive oil. Cook until browned.

6. Add pasta, zucchini, and mushrooms to cream sauce, stirring for 1 minute.

7. Serve by topping with Parmesan cheese!

BEER MAKES EVERYTHING BETTER

Avocado Eggrolls
with Mustard Pale Ale Sauce

Serves 2–4

The hop and mustard flavor in the sauce pairs perfectly with the egg rolls.

Ingredients:

1 avocado, diced
¼ cup red onion, thinly
  diced
½ cup roasted red pepper,
  chopped
1 tablespoon jalapeños,
  seeded and diced
½ teaspoon lime juice
½ teaspoon cilantro
½ teaspoon salt
¼ teaspoon pepper
Egg roll wrappers

Directions:

1. Preheat oven to 400°F.

2. In medium bowl combine avocado, red onion, red pepper, jalapeños, lime juice, cilantro, salt and pepper.

3. Spoon small amount of filling onto egg roll wrappers.

4. Use a brush (or your finger) to lightly wet edges with water. Fold to make a triangle.

5. Place parchment paper on sheet pan and spray with cooking spray.

6. Add egg rolls and brush with olive oil.

7. Bake for 10–15 minutes.

8. Slice in half diagonally and serve with Mustard Pale Ale Sauce (page 48).

PRO TIP

Serve with Mustard Pale Ale Sauce for a spicy Asian flavor, or serve with sour cream and salsa for a more traditional taste.

Pale Ale Pizza Crust

Serves 2

We all know a cold beer goes great with pizza. Adding beer to the crust takes it to a whole new level.

Ingredients:

3 cups flour
Salt
1 cup pale ale
Olive oil
Pizza sauce
Pizza toppings of choice

Directions:

1. Mix flour, salt, and beer in medium bowl.

2. Form into a ball. Make sure all flour is thoroughly mixed and dough is workable and not too dry. Add more beer if necessary.

3. Cover bowl with towel and let rise for 10 minutes.

4. Preheat oven to 425°F.

5. Use a small amount of oil to lightly coat baking sheet or pizza stone.

6. Spread dough out on baking sheet or pizza stone. Poke dough with fork every 1–2 inches. Cook in oven for 5–10 minutes before topping.

7. Remove and top with sauce, cheese, and other toppings of choice.

8. Bake for 8–12 more minutes, or until dough is cooked and toppings are done.

Ultimate Grilled 3 Cheese with Mustard Pale Ale Sauce

Serves 1

This super cheesy sandwich goes nicely with the beer-infused Pale Ale Sauce.

Ingredients:

Butter
2 bread slices
1 slice Swiss
1 slice Colby-Jack
1 slice cheddar
Pickles
Mustard Pale Ale sauce
   (page 48)

Directions:

1. Lightly butter bread on each side.

2. Add cheese slices.

3. Cook in a medium pan, covered, on medium-low heat until bread is golden brown and cheese is melted.

4. Open sandwich and add pickles.

5. Cut into 1–2-inch strips and dip in Pale Ale sauce.

Easy Peasey Beer Bread

Makes 1 loaf

I like to use porters for this recipe. A dark, chocolaty beer gives the bread a rich flavor.

Ingredients:

3 cups self-rising flour
3 tablespoons sugar
1 beer
1 teaspoon butter

Directions:

1. Mix flour and sugar together in a large bowl.

2. Stir in beer, making sure all the dry ingredients are fully mixed.

3. Transfer to a greased loaf pan.

4. Cook for 45–60 minutes at 350°F.

5. Remove from oven and brush top of loaf with butter.

6. Slice and eat!

Pale Ale Pub Fries

Serves 2–4

Here is another great way to use my soon-to-be-famous Mustard Pale Ale Sauce.

Ingredients:

1 bag of frozen steak fries
Salt and pepper to taste
¼ cup bacon (optional)
1 cup Colby-Jack cheese, shredded
1 jalapeño, sliced
Mustard Pale Ale Sauce (page 48)

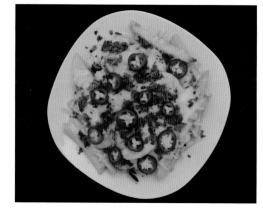

Directions:

1. Cook the fries in the oven using the directions on the package. Remove from oven and salt and pepper to taste. Place in an oven-safe dish.

2. Cook bacon to a crispy light brown in skillet over medium-high heat. Once cooked, put on a paper towel-lined plate to allow some grease to soak up. Chop into small bits.

3. Layer cheese on a pile of fries.

4. Place in oven set to broil at 350°F.

5. Leave in oven until cheese melts, 3–5 minutes. Be careful not to let the cheese burn!

6. Remove from oven and top with jalapeños and bacon.

BEER BELLY BUSTER

Use turkey bacon. It is lower in fat and a bit healthier!

7. Serve with a side of Mustard Pale Ale Sauce!

BBQ Basted Shrimp Kabobs

Serves 2–4

This is a summer grilling favorite of mine. Grab a beer, fire up the grill, and get your BBQ on!

Ingredients:

1 tablespoon olive oil
1 pound of raw shrimp,
    small (26–30 count size)
Metal or wooden skewers
IPA BBQ Sauce (page 29)

Shrimp directions:

1. Put raw shrimp on skewer. Brush with very small amount of olive oil.

2. Grill on charcoal or gas grill for 1–2 minutes (just long enough to give it grill marks), then flip. Brush shrimp kabobs with sauce after turning.

3. Cook an additional 4–5 minutes per side or until cooked through.

4. Remove from skewers. Serve with side of BBQ sauce.

Sautéed Cerveza Scallops with Corn Salsa

Serves 2

Best served with a cold Mexican beer.

Ingredients:

Scallops:
1 clove garlic, chopped
1 tablespoon butter
1 Mexican beer
12 ounces large sea scallops
Salt and pepper
Dash of cayenne
Lime wedge

Corn salsa:
½ cup corn, drained
½ cup black beans, rinsed
    and drained
¼ cup red onions, diced
1 jalapeño, diced
1 tablespoon cilantro,
    chopped
Juice of 1 lime
Salt and pepper to taste

Directions for scallops:

1. In a large pan, sauté the garlic in 1 tablespoon butter for one minute.

2. Add splash of beer to pan.

3. Season scallops with salt, pepper, and dash of cayenne. Sauté scallops in pan 2–3 minutes per side.

4. Once scallops are done, remove from pan, lower heat, and add beer.

5. Stir for 3–5 minutes on low heat; just enough to infuse the beer with the pan seasonings to make a sauce.

6. Squeeze the lime wedge to top it off.

7. Serve with a scoop of the corn salsa and a handful of corn chips.

Directions for salsa:

1. Combine all ingredients in small bowl.

Cocktail Shrimp
with John's Killer Cocktail Sauce

Serves 2–4

I have been making cocktail sauce for over twenty years. Ever since I worked as a busboy at the Springfield Inn restaurant. This is the culmination of all those years of experience. The perfect blend of tang and heat.

Ingredients:

1 pound of cooked cocktail shrimp, 16–25 count "jumbo"

John's Killer cocktail sauce:
½ cup ketchup
1 teaspoon Worcestershire sauce
1 tablespoon horseradish, raw (more if you want it extra "killer")
Dash of hot sauce
½ teaspoon lemon juice
½ teaspoon gose beer
1 teaspoon steak sauce (optional)

Directions:

1. Combine all ingredients in small bowl.

2. Taste and add more horseradish if you want an extra kick.

3. Dip chilled shrimp in sauce and enjoy!

Potato Skin Pizza

Serves 2

With my wife's help, I turned a classic Happy Hour dish into one of the best pizzas I have ever made.

Ingredients:

3 cups flour
Salt
1 cup beer
Olive oil
2 baked potatoes
2 tablespoons butter
  to fry potatoes
4–6 strips of bacon
Shredded Colby-Jack
  cheese
Green onions,
  chopped
Ranch dressing

Directions:

1. Mix flour, salt, and beer in medium bowl.

2. Form into a ball. Make sure all flour is thoroughly mixed and dough is workable and not too dry. Add more beer if necessary. Cover bowl with towel and let rise for 10 minutes.

3. Preheat oven to 425°F.

4. Use small amount of oil to lightly coat baking sheet or pizza stone.

5. Spread dough out on baking sheet or pizza stone. Poke dough with fork every 1–2 inches.

6. Cook in oven for 5–10 minutes before topping.

7. Chop 2 medium baked potatoes into cubes. Fry in medium pan using butter until brown on each side.

8. Cook bacon until crispy on each side. Chop into bits.

9. Remove dough from the oven and top with potatoes, cheese, and bacon. Bake for another 8–12 minutes or until dough is cooked and toppings are done.

10. Add green onions and dip in ranch dressing.

BEER BELLY BUSTER

Use turkey bacon instead of regular bacon to cut down on the fat.

Great Food Pairings

"Without question, the greatest invention in the history of mankind is beer. Oh, I grant you that the wheel was also a fine invention, but the wheel does not go nearly as well with pizza."
—Dave Barry

Tilapia and Broccoli with Stella

Serves 2

The light fish and broccoli pair nicely with this crisp Belgian pilsner. Like my favorite Irish rock band Homeland, I believe Stella is best drank on a Sunday.

Ingredients:

4 medium pieces of tilapia
Old Bay seasoning
1 crown of broccoli
1 teaspoon butter
Salt and pepper to taste
Lemon wedge

Directions:

1. Season fish with Old Bay and cook using olive oil in medium sauté pan. Flip after 3–5 minutes, when the side is light brown and crispy.

2. Steam broccoli in pan steamer. Remove from steamer, add butter, salt, and pepper. (Or cook broccoli in a plastic container: add butter, salt, and pepper then microwave on high for 2–3 minutes.)

3. Put 2 pieces of tilapia per plate and split the broccoli.

4. Squeeze lemon over both. Serve with a nice pilsner!

Pan-Fried Cheese Rangoons with an American Lager

Serves 2

Here's the deal. I tried to bake these, but the wrappers weren't crisp and they lacked flavor. Then I pan-fried them and they were so good, the wife and I polished off a batch hovering over the countertop. That's how you know this recipe is a winner.

Ingredients:

1 (8-ounce) package cream cheese, softened to room temperature

3 green onions, chopped, whites discarded

½ teaspoon garlic powder

¼ teaspoon sea salt

Cracked black pepper (several grinds)

1 package wonton wrappers

Water for brushing wrappers

Oil for frying (grapeseed, coconut, or canola)

Directions:

1. Once cream cheese is softened, mix in onions, garlic powder, salt, and black pepper. Add seasoning to taste.

2. Pile a teaspoon of filling into the center of a wonton wrapper, then brush the water on the outer edge of all four sides of the wrapper and press to close. Be sure not to overfill the wrapper or your filling will come out while cooking. Repeat this step until all filling is used.

3. Heat 3–4 tablespoons of oil in a large non-stick pan over medium-high heat until a drop of water splatters in the pan.

4. Pan fry the wontons 5–6 per batch, careful not to overcrowd. After about a minute, flip and fry other side. They should be golden brown. Lay the finished fried wontons on paper towels to drain and repeat until the rest of the wontons are fried.

5. To eat, serve with pepper jelly or sweet chili sauce.

BEER BELLY BUSTER

Use non-dairy cream cheese like Tofutti brand. It tastes just as good!

Swordfish with Mango Salsa and Summer Ale

Serves 2

A nice mild beer like Sam Adams Summer Ale pairs nicely with the steak-like texture of the swordfish.

Ingredients:

2 swordfish steaks
1 tablespoon olive oil
Old Bay seasoning
2 mangos, diced
1 jalapeños
½ red onion diced
¼ cup fresh cilantro chopped
1 lime for juice
Salt and pepper

Directions:

1. Brush swordfish with olive oil and season with Old Bay seasoning.

2. Grill 4–5 minutes per side or until done, but not dry.

3. Dice mangos, jalapeño, onion, and cilantro. In medium bowl, combine with juice of 1 lime and lightly season with salt and pepper to taste.

4. Serve swordfish topped with salsa.

BEER MAKES EVERYTHING BETTER

Pasta with Clam Sauce and White Wine

Serves 2

Next time your friends stop by and leave a partially drank bottle of wine you will know exactly what to do with it.

Ingredients:

1 pound fettuccine pasta
1 tablespoon olive oil
½ white onion, diced
2 garlic cloves, minced
1 pound clams
1 cup white wine
Handful fresh parsley,
    chopped
1 tablespoon butter
Salt and pepper
¼ teaspoon cayenne pepper
Lemon zest to taste

Directions:

1. Cook pasta according to package (al dente works best).

2. Heat the olive oil in a large sauté pan. Add onion and garlic and sauté until soft, about 2 to 4 minutes. Be careful not to burn the garlic.

3. Add the clams and wine. Cover and simmer for 6 to 8 minutes or until most of the clams are cooked. You will know they are finished when the shells open up.

4. Add 2 tablespoons chopped parsley, salt, pepper, and cayenne, and stir in the butter. Cook for a few more minutes to thicken the sauce.

5. Drain pasta and add to sauté pan and mix. Pour pasta into large serving bowl.

6. Zest lemon over the dish. Garnish with remaining parsley. Serve immediately.

Spring Salad with (or without) Chicken with Blue Moon

Serves 2

A salad is the perfect pairing for a light, refreshing summer ale. Summer ales are fruity wheat beers and work perfect with a spring mixed salad.

Ingredients:

1 bag spring mix salad
Dried cranberries
Walnuts, chopped
Orange, chopped into small pieces
Goat cheese, crumbled
1 chicken breast

Directions:

1. Use pre-packaged spring salad mix and add dried cranberries, chopped walnuts, orange pieces, and goat cheese. Toss with vinaigrette dressing or poppy seed dressing—something light or fruity.

2. Cook chicken breast in small pan over medium heat in olive oil. Make sure to cook through.

3. Slice chicken and top salad. Enjoy with or without extra dressing.

BEER MAKES EVERYTHING BETTER

Pizza and PBR

Serves 1–2

This recipe is dedicated to my brother-in-law Nick, who we nickname Captain PBR.

Ingredients:

Phone
Local pizza joint phone
    number
3–6 Cans of PBR

Directions:

1. Pick up the phone and call your favorite pizza delivery place.

2. Order your favorite pizza pie.

3. Crack open a PBR while you wait for your pizza to arrive.

4. When pizza arrives, tip generously.

5. Once the can is empty, open new can and start sipping.

6. Repeat until desired outcome is achieved.

Easy Bean Burritos with Pacifico

Serves 2

Keep a can of refried beans in your pantry so that you're ready whenever you have a hankering for running for the border.

Ingredients:

Can of refried beans
2 Tortillas
Shredded lettuce
Salsa
Sour cream
Taco seasoning
Beer
Lime

Directions:

1. Crack open Pacifico, squeeze lime in glass, and pour beer into a glass.

2. Warm the refried beans in a pot on the stove top and add taco seasoning (if the beans are not already seasoned).

3. In large skillet, heat tortillas. Add all ingredients to tortilla and roll.

4. Drizzle lime over top and enjoy!

Cheese Quesadillas with Tecate or Dos Equis

Serves 1–2

This is a quick meal for one or snack for two. Pair with a cold Mexican beer for a winning combination.

Ingredients:

2 tortillas
½ cup shredded Colby-Jack cheese
1 jalapeño, sliced (optional)
Sour cream
Salsa
Lime
Beer

Directions:

1. Warm large pan (make sure it is big enough to fit tortillas). Place tortilla in pan.

2. Sprinkle cheese and jalapeño on tortilla. Heat until cheese melts.

3. Fold in half, remove from pan and cut into slices using a pizza cutter (or knife).

4. Repeat steps 2–5 for second tortilla.

5. Serve with a dollop of sour cream and salsa. Crack open Mexican-style beer and add lime wedge. Enjoy!

Mahi Reuben with Little Sumpin' Sumpin' Ale

Makes 2 sandwiches

I had my first Mahi Reuben on a weekend trip to Put-in-Bay. This wonderful sandwich pairs great with a mild IPA.

Ingredients:

Thousand Island sauce:
2 tablespoons ketchup
2 tablespoons mayo
1 tablespoon pickle relish
1 tablespoon pure
   horseradish
Dash of salt and black
   pepper

1 piece (4 ounces) Mahi
Blackening (or Old Bay)
   seasoning
Butter
4 slices rye bread
2–4 slices Swiss cheese
Pickles
4 or more tablespoons
   sauerkraut, drained

Directions for sauce:

1. Stir to combine

Directions for Mahi:

1. Heat medium pan on medium high. Add olive oil (just enough to lightly coat the pan).

2. Season Mahi with a generous amount of Old Bay seasoning or other favorite blackening seasoning.

3. Grill on each side for 4–5 minutes; don't overcook and dry out.

Continued on page 68.

Sandwich:

1. Once you start the Mahi, butter one side each of the 4 pieces of rye bread.

2. Heat large pan to medium-high and grill bread with Swiss cheese inside for 3–4 minutes each or until golden brown and the cheese is melty. You can use 1 slice per sandwich or kick it up with 2 per for extra cheesiness.

3. Once Mahi is cooked and sandwich is finished, pull apart bread and add pickles, drained Sauerkraut, half of the Mahi per sandwich, and Thousand Island sauce.

Slice in half and enjoy!

BEER MAKES EVERYTHING BETTER

Black Bean Tacos with Negra Modelo or Dos Equis

Serves 2

Tacos and beer, need I say more?

Ingredients:

1 can black beans
Hard taco shells
Colby-Jack cheese, shredded
1 can corn
Sour cream
Lettuce, shredded

Directions:

1. Heat black beans in pot and partially mash, if desired.

2. Heat taco shells in oven for 5 minutes at 350°F or until warm but not burnt.

3. For best results, layer taco in this order: beans, cheese, corn, sour cream, and lettuce.

4. Lean head to the right and insert taco into mouth vertically. Repeat until taco is gone.

5. Drink beer with lime when mouth seems dry or refreshment is needed.

Smoked Salmon, Goat Cheese, and Crackers with Smoked Porter

Serves 2

If you are not able to find a smoked porter, don't worry. Salmon and goat cheese taste great with most porters. The Packard Porter on page 120 is a great substitute.

Ingredients:

Smoked salmon
Goat cheese
Your favorite crackers
A mild smoked porter

Directions:

1. Slice up the salmon and cheese on a small plate.

2. Or sit down at the table with all the packages, a plate, and a cheese knife, and start piling up crackers. I use a ratio of 50% toppings and 50% cracker but you can mix it up any way you like.

Gruyere Cheese Plate with Lake Erie Monster or Other Double/Imperial IPA

Serves 2–4

Strong hoppy beers pair nicely with strong-tasting cheeses. Gruyere, cheddar, and even an aged Swiss work well. Cheese plates are all about the presentation.

Ingredients:
Various cheese selections
Crackers
Beer

Directions:

1. Use a rectangle shaped plate and arrange the crackers and cheese in rows from top to bottom of the short side of the plate.

2. Cut the cheese into medium to small squares and layer in a diamond shape, stacking one on the other.

3. Use very mild crackers and eat them in between samples to cleanse your pallet.

PRO TIP

For an extra fun night have a selection of IPAs available to have more of a beer tasting.

Leftover Halloween Candy Paired with Oktoberfest Ale

On Halloween in our neighborhood we stand on our porch, drink beer, and hand out candy to kids in costumes.

Ingredients:

Halloween candy
Your favorite Oktoberfest
   beer

Directions:

1. Steal a handful of candy from your kids' Halloween basket (Hey, they don't need the extra sugar anyway).

2. Eat candy and drink beer.

PRO TIP

The chocolatey candy works best but don't be scared to try something different. Smarties taste surprisingly good with beer!

BEER MAKES EVERYTHING BETTER

Sunday Morning Helpers

"I feel sorry for people who don't drink. When they wake up in the morning, that's as good as they're going to feel all day."
—Frank Sinatra

After a rough Saturday night, these meals will help get you back to the land of the living.

Hangover Hash for Two

Serves 2

Being married to a famous romance author has its perks. This recipe was created by one of my wife's book heroes, Evan. It is so good that I wanted you to see it in my book.

Ingredients:

4–5 new red potatoes, scrubbed and rinsed
¼ of a green pepper, cubed
¼ of a sweet Vidalia onion, cubed
1 tablespoon olive oil
2 eggs
2 slices multi-grain bread
Sharp cheddar cheese

Directions:

1. Place potatoes in a pot and cover with cold water. Put a lid on the pot and bring to a boil. Once boiling, remove the lid and continue to cook the potatoes for 12–14 minutes or until you can stick the tip of a knife in a potato, and it slips off the edge.

2. Remove from water and cut into cubes.

3. Put a drizzle of olive oil in a large frying pan and toss in cubed potatoes, green pepper, and onions. Cook over medium-high heat, tossing on occasion.

4. Put a drizzle of olive oil in a small frying pan and heat over medium-high. Crack two eggs into the pan and immediately lower the heat to medium. Flip so as not to break the yolk.

5. Make toast. Butter toast.

6. Pile red potatoes, onions, and green peppers onto the center of your plate, sprinkle on sharp cheddar cheese, and layer egg on top.

Toad in the Hole

Serves 1–2

When I was growing up, my mom used to make this twist on eggs and toast.

Ingredients:

2 eggs
2 pieces of bread
Butter
Salt, pepper, and cayenne to
taste

PRO TIP

Use different shaped
cookie cutters for different
occasions, like a clover for
Saint Patty's Day.

Directions:

1. Use cookie cutter to cut center out of bread.

2. Heat large pan to medium-high heat. Melt the butter, then place bread in pan (including center section), and crack an egg into the empty part of bread.

3. Lower heat to medium and flip bread once it is toasted and egg whites are turning solid. The idea is to keep the egg yolk soft and the whites solid. Season to taste.

4. Plate with center bread piece on top of the egg.

5. Eat by cutting into egg and dipping center bread in soft yoke then cut bread into bite-sized pieces.

Banana, Spinach, Honey Smoothie

Serves 1–2

The perfect quick and healthy breakfast to get your day started right.

Ingredients:

½ cup water
½ cup milk
1 banana
1 cup fresh baby spinach
1 tablespoon honey
1 tablespoon lemon juice
1 teaspoon protein powder
(optional)
Ice cubes

Directions:

1. Combine all ingredients in blender and mix on medium high until smooth.

2. Pour into glass and drink slowly.

BEER BELLY BUSTER

Use non-dairy milk (like almond milk) as a healthier option.

75

Avocado and Cheese Omelet

Serves 2

The fat in the avocado and protein in the eggs is perfect to help you recover after a long night out.

Ingredients:

3–4 eggs
2 tablespoons milk
Salt and pepper
Dash of cayenne pepper
2 slices bread for toast
   (I like a nice medium
   wheat bread myself)
½ avocado
Cheddar cheese, shredded
Bacon bits (optional)
1 teaspoon butter

Directions:

1. Crack the eggs in a bowl, add milk, and whisk to combine.

2. Use a large pan with a lid. Heat to medium low and melt the butter. Add egg mixture to the warm pan, making sure the pan does not get too hot (The plan is to cook the eggs very slowly and not let them brown on one side.)

3. Top with salt, pepper, and cayenne, then cover. Turn the burner down to low and let it cook until the eggs are no longer runny, 5–10 minutes.

4. Meanwhile, start toasting bread and dice the avocado.

5. Once the eggs are almost completely cooked, sprinkle the avocado, cheese, and bacon bits on half of the eggs. Cover and let heat until the cheese is melted, 1–2 minutes.

6. Once the cheese is melted, fold the omelet in half using the side with no toppings.

7. Cut in half and serve with your toast.

Eggs Spinidict

Serves 2

This is the go-to breakfast in the Lemmon household. Checkout my website www.thathappyhourguy.com for an instructional video for this recipe.

Ingredients:

1–2 cups fresh spinach
2 eggs
½ teaspoon butter
Salt and pepper, or your
    favorite egg seasoning
    (I love Fox Point from
    Penzey's Spices)
2 pieces wheat bread
½ avocado

Directions:

1. Wilt spinach in covered pan using a small amount of water or olive oil.

2. Cook eggs over medium heat in pan using butter and seasoning.

3. Toast bread and spread ¼ of the avocado on each side.

4. Add ½ the wilted spinach to each and top with the egg.

CHAPTER 8

THERE'S A PORTER IN MY PANCAKES— BEER FOR DESSERT

"Any man who eats dessert is not drinking enough."
—Ernest Hemingway

This chapter will teach you to satisfy your sweet tooth by adding beer to some sweeter fare. It is always best to finish your Happy Hour with something sweet. You might be thinking, "Pancakes aren't dessert!" Maybe that is true, but if you can have pancakes for dinner, why not have them for dessert? Since I added beer to the pancakes, you could even make Happy Hour for breakfast.

Devil Dog Cupcakes

Makes 12–14

I borrowed this recipe from my famous romance author wife. Her favorite part is that this recipe is vegan but non-vegans will never guess.

Cupcakes:

1½ cups flour
1 cup sugar
½ cup cocoa powder
1 teaspoon baking soda
½ teaspoon salt
½ cup coconut oil, melted
1 tablespoon apple cider
   vinegar
2 teaspoons vanilla
1 can coconut milk

Cupcake Directions:

1. Preheat oven to 350°F. Line a 12-cup muffin tin with cupcake liners.

2. Whisk flour, sugar, cocoa powder, soda, and salt, into a large bowl.

3. In a separate bowl, combine oil, vinegar, vanilla, and coconut milk.

4. Add wet ingredients to dry and stir until just combined. Do not overmix.

5. Fill cupcake liners about ⅔ of the way full. If you have leftover batter, line a few cups in another tin, or just eat the batter.

6. Bake 16–20 minutes or until toothpick comes out dry.

Vanilla Frosting:

1 cup non-hydrogenated
   vegetable shortening
3 cups powdered sugar
2 teaspoons vanilla
3–5 tablespoons non-dairy
   milk

Frosting Directions:

1. Using beaters or a stand mixer, beat vegetable shortening, adding powdered sugar a cup at a time. When mixture becomes dry, add non-dairy milk a tablespoon at a time.

2. Continue adding sugar until all three cups have been added. Stir in vanilla. Scrape down the sides with a rubber spatula as needed.

3. Spoon frosting into a large plastic bag (or a frosting bag), twist, and cut the corner off. Set aside.

Chocolate Wine Sauce*:

¼ cup non-dairy creamer (or
   milk)
¼ cup red wine
1 cup chocolate chips

Wine Sauce Directions:

1. Warm the creamer or milk over the stove until simmering (but not boiling) and transfer to a bowl.

2. Stir in chocolate chips to melt (it takes time, so be patient), while warming the wine on the stove to simmering. Once wine is warmed, add to the chocolate mixture.

3. Continue stirring until smooth. If the chips are not melting, pop bowl into the microwave for 15 seconds and stir. Repeat if necessary until sauce is smooth and glossy.

*I couldn't resist adding wine to the chocolate sauce. If you don't want the wine, simply swap out for a stout or extra creamer if you are all out of booze. Leftover chocolate sauce will solidify in the fridge, but will melt in a few seconds in the microwave.

To assemble:

1. Once cupcakes are cooled completely (good luck—I ate one warm), unwrap from cupcake liner and put on a plate.
2. Pipe a generous mountain of frosting on the top, then spoon on the chocolate sauce. Top with a tiny bit of frosting and a maraschino cherry, if desired.
3. Enjoy with a fork and a smile . . . preferably at your next Girls' Night Out or Happy Hour at Home.

There's a Porter in My Pancakes

Serves 2–4

The Packard Porter from page 120 is perfect for this quick breakfast treat.

Ingredients:

1 cup flour
1 tablespoon baking powder
1 teaspoon sugar
⅛ teaspoon salt
½ cup water
½ cup porter beer
½ teaspoon vanilla extract
¼ cup chocolate chips
Cooking spray to coat pan or griddle
Butter, peanut butter, or maple syrup to taste

Directions:

1. Whisk together flour, baking soda, sugar, and salt in a large mixing bowl.

2. Stir together water, beer, and vanilla extract in separate small mixing bowl.

3. Slowly stir in the wet mixture into the dry and make sure not to over stir (Some lumps are okay).

4. Add chocolate chips and stir to combine.

5. Use ¼-cup measuring cup to scoop pancake mixture onto lightly greased large pan or griddle using medium-high heat.

6. After a few minutes and once the bubbles stop, flip and continue to cook until golden brown.

7. Serve with butter and maple syrup to taste.

PRO TIP

You could also spread peanut butter on your pancakes to make them extra rich and add some protein.

Smitty's Hot Fudge Stout Sauce

Makes 2 cups

The stout complements the rich flavor of the chocolate. Beer plus chocolate is a sure winner.

Ingredients:

½ cup heavy cream

1 tablespoon butter

⅓ cup stout (An Imperial Stout works well but I use Guinness or Grampa Grimm's ⅛ Irish Stout myself)

1 cup semi-sweet chocolate chips

Directions:

1. Slowly warm up the butter and cream in large pan on medium-low heat. Make sure not to let it get too hot.

2. Measure beer (drink the leftover while you wait for the butter and cream to heat). Next, stir in the beer.

3. Once that is combined and warm, slowly start stirring in the chocolate chips a few at a time.

4. Once the chocolate chips are melted, remove from heat and let cool. The sauce will thicken as it cools.

5. Pour over ice cream, dip sliced fruit (apples and pears work great), or just eat with a spoon.

Floating Away: Beer Floats

Serves 1

There are many beers that taste good when served with ice cream. I tend to like chocolate stouts or porters the best myself. Grampa Grimm's Packard Porter makes a great float! I am a big fan of vanilla ice cream but you could use chocolate or any other of your favorite types. Feel free to try different combinations of beer and ice cream. Leave me a note on social media to let me know your favorite concoction.

Ingredients:

1 beer
2 small scoops of ice cream

Directions:

1. Pour beer into large mug (a 20-ounce mug works well).

2. Let beer sit for a minute to let the foam go down.

3. Softly place 2 small scoops of ice cream in beer mug. Enjoy with a spoon.

PRO TIP

This recipe works really well with hard root beer like Not Your Father's Root Beer.

Stout Chocolate Chip Cookies

Makes 20–24 cookies

The bitterness of a stout works nicely to balance the sweetness of the sugar.

Ingredients:

2½ cups all-purpose flour
½ teaspoon baking powder
¾ teaspoon cinnamon
¼ teaspoon salt
½ tablespoon espresso powder (or 1 packet Starbucks VIA Ready Brew)
1 cup coconut oil (keeps the cookies soft when storing)
1 cup powdered sugar
½ cup brown sugar
4 ounces (½ cup) stout beer (an oatmeal stout works even better)
1 cup chocolate cups

Directions:

1. Preheat oven to 350°F.

2. Hand whisk flour, baking powder, cinnamon, salt, and espresso powder in medium bowl.

3. Use hand mixer (or a spoon) to mix coconut oil, both sugars, and the beer in a separate medium mixing bowl. Once this is thoroughly combined, start mixing in the dry ingredients slowly until all the batter is smooth.

4. Use a wooden spoon (or your hands) to "fold" in the chocolate chips.

5. Use a tablespoon or small scooper and put small scoops on a lightly greased baking sheet (I like to smash the round balls a little to flatten them out and help them cook more evenly).

6. Bake at 350°F for 18–20 minutes or until light golden brown.

PRO TIP

To make them a little sweeter, sprinkle a small amount of regular white sugar on each cookie as they cool. This will also give a nicer presentation.

BEER BELLY BUSTER

Don't tell anyone but these great tasting cookies are dairy-free, egg-free, and 99 percent vegan.

CHAPTER 9

Fancy it Up—Beer Cocktails

"I drink too much. Last time I gave a urine sample, it had an olive in it.
—Rodney Dangerfield

Whether you hold your pinky up and look sophisticated drinking out of a rocks glass or use this as the "gateway drug" to your non-drinking buddies, beer cocktails are a great Happy Hour addition. My beer cocktail ideas started when my wife was craving a mojito and we were (sadly) all out of rum. But, we *did* have fresh mint from our garden, blueberries in the freezer and some of my latest light brew, the Great Scot 60 Shilling Ale. I had to improvise to keep the lady of the house happy and the results were all kinds of awesome—beer-infused cocktails! Cause once we started mixing, we couldn't stop. Beer cocktails prove that beer mixed with some great cocktail ingredients can taste incredible. Want a mint julep for a race day Happy Hour but don't like gin? Or do you think old fashioneds are only for men over sixty? Think again.

When mixing up these fancy cocktails you will have some leftover beer. I suggest you start a second cocktail or drink the remainder while you are making it!

Beer Cocktail Recipes

Blueberry Mojito

Serving size = (1) 8–10 ounce cocktail

I love using fresh mint from my garden for this cocktail. Mint is a perennial and grows easily in most climates.

Ingredients:

1 light to medium beer
   (lagers or light ales work
   nicely)
2 ounces fresh blueberries
½ teaspoon sugar
1 lime wedge
3–5 mint leaves

Directions:

1. Pour a few ounces of beer in the glass and add the blueberries, sugar, lime, and mint leaves. Using a muddler (or end of a large wooden spoon), smash and mix the contents together. (Make sure you smash the blueberries and lime well to release the juices.) Use a regular spoon if necessary to mix thoroughly.

2. Next, add a few ice cubes. Pour approximately 4–6 ounces of beer slowly over the ice (you don't want it to foam too much, or it'll go flat).

3. Give the cocktail one final stir. Garnish with mint leaf and enjoy!

Strawberry Basil Blast

Serving size = (1) 8–10 ounce cocktail served in a rocks glass.

The fruity strawberry mixes well with the sweet basil for a wonderful blend.

Ingredients:

8 ounces light to medium beer (lagers or light ales work nicely)

2 ounces of fresh strawberries

1 wedge of lime

½ teaspoon sugar

3–5 small basil leaves

Directions:

1. Pour a few ounces of beer in the glass and add the strawberries, lime, sugar, and basil leaves. Using a muddler (or end of a large wooden spoon), smash and mix the contents together. (Make sure you smash the strawberries and lime well to release the juices.) Use a regular spoon if necessary to mix thoroughly.

2. Next, add a few ice cubes. Pour approximately 4–6 ounces of beer slowly over the ice (you don't want it to foam too much, or it'll go flat).

3. Give the cocktail one final stir. Garnish with basil leaf and strawberry.

PRO TIP

You could also use a "martini" shaker to mash, mix, and strain with ice into your cocktail glass before filling with beer. This will strain out the floating leaves, ice, and strawberry pieces and give a clearer appearance.

Stirred Not Shaken Beertini

Serving size = (1) 8–10 ounce cocktail served in a rocks glass, or strain the ice and pour in a martini glass.

James Bond would love this fancy fake out.

Ingredients:

6 ounces light to medium beer (lagers or light ales work nicely)

1 ounce of your favorite vodka

3–5 olives

1 ounce of blue cheese crumbles

1 twist of lemon

Directions:

1. Pour ½ the beer in the glass and add the vodka and ice. Stir slowly.

2. Remove the pimentos from the olives and stuff the blue cheese crumbles inside.

3. Use the rind side of the lemon twist and rub it around the rim of the glass.

4. Garnish with the olives on a tooth pick and enjoy!

Beer-A-Rita

Serving size = (1) 8–10 ounce cocktail served in a rocks glass or a margarita glass like in the picture.

This cocktail is perfect for when you can't decide between having a beer or a margarita.

Ingredients:

Coarse salt
1 lime wedge
8 ounces light Mexican beer
1 ounce of your favorite
   tequila

Directions:

1. Fill shot glass with tequila, lick part of hand between thumb and pointer finger, sprinkle with salt, lick salt off hand, drink shot of tequila, and suck on lime wedge. Continue to make beer cocktail.

2. Pour small amount of coarse salt on plate. Run lime wedge around top edge of glass. Carefully dip glass in salt.

3. Pour beer in the glass, squeeze lime wedge, add tequila and ice.

4. Stir slowly.

5. Garnish with a lime wedge.

Harvey's Beer Banger

Serving size = (1) 8–10 ounce cocktail served in a rocks glass.

You will love this take on the old Harvey Wall Banger I used to serve back in the day at the Springfield Country Club.

Ingredients:

6–8 ounces light to medium beer (lagers or light ales work nicely)
1 orange slice
1 ounce of Galliano (or other orange flavored liqueur)
½ teaspoon sugar
1 twist of orange

Directions:

1. Pour a few ounces of beer in the glass, and add the orange wedge and sugar. Using a muddler (or end of a large wooden spoon), smash and mix the contents together making sure to smash the orange well.

2. Pour beer in the glass, add the Galliano and ice. Stir slowly.

3. Use the rind side of the orange twist and rub it around the rim of the glass.

4. Garnish with the twist and enjoy!

Beer-mosa

Serving size = (1) 12 ounce cocktail served in a cocktail or beer glass.

This cocktail is perfect if you prefer beer over champagne.

Ingredients:

6 ounces wheat beer
1 ounce of your favorite vodka (optional)
4 ounces of orange juice (fresh squeezed is best)
1 orange wedge

Directions:

1. Pour beer in the glass, add the vodka, orange juice, and ice. Stir slowly.

2. Garnish with the orange wedge and enjoy!

PRO TIP

This makes for a great brunch or early daytime beverage.

Sangria

Serving size = (1) large wine glass.

Ingredients:

1 glass of sweet red wine
  (yes wine, no beer for
  this one)
1 orange wedge
1 lime wedge
2–4 maraschino cherries

Directions:

1. Pour a few ounces of wine in a glass. Add the orange, lime, and cherries. Using a muddler (or the end of a large wooden spoon), smash and mix the contents together.

2. Pour this and the wine into the large wine glass and add a few ice cubes (optional). Stir slowly.

3. Garnish with an orange wedge, lime wedge, and a cherry on a toothpick and enjoy!

Note: Depending on how sweet the red wine you choose you may want to add some sugar to sweeten it up.

Raspberry Limeade

Serving size = (1) 8–10 ounce cocktail served in a "tall" cocktail glass.

Raspberry and lime go together nicely in this fruity cocktail.

Ingredients:

6–8 ounces light to medium beer (lagers or light ales work nicely)
2 ounces of fresh raspberries
1 teaspoon sugar
2 wedges of lime

Directions:

1. Pour a few ounces of beer in the glass and add the raspberries and sugar, and squeeze both lime wedges. Using a muddler (or the end of a large wooden spoon), smash and mix the contents together. Stir until the sugar is dissolved.

2. Next, add a few ice cubes. Pour approximately 4–6 ounces of beer slowly over the ice.

3. Give the cocktail one final stir. Garnish with a lime.

Note: This recipe works well with blackberries or mulberries so use your favorite or mix and match.

Beer Fashioned

Serving size = (1) 8–10 ounce cocktail served in a rocks glass, or strain the ice and pour in a martini glass.

This is my beer-infused version of the classic Old Fashioned.

Ingredients:

6 ounces medium ale beer
1 orange wedge
1 cherry
½ teaspoon sugar
Dash of bitters (optional)

Directions:

1. Pour a few ounces of beer in the glass. Add orange, cherry, sugar, and bitters (optional). Using a muddler (or end of a large wooden spoon), smash and mix the contents together. Use a regular spoon if necessary to mix thoroughly and make sure the sugar is dissolved.

2. Next, add a few ice cubes. Pour approximately 4–6 ounces of beer slowly over the ice.

3. Strain into a martini glass if serving "up."

4. Give the cocktail one final stir.

5. Garnish with a "flag" (an orange wedge folded around a cherry with a toothpick through it).

Mint Julep

Serving size = (1) 8–10 ounce cocktail served in a rocks glass.

The perfect cocktail to serve up at your next Kentucky Derby party. Just make sure you wear a large hat!

Ingredients:

6–8 ounces light lager beer
1 lime wedge
3–5 fresh mint leaves
1 teaspoon powdered sugar

Directions:

1. Pour a few ounces of beer in the glass. Add lime, mint, and sugar. Using a muddler (or end of a large wooden spoon), smash and mix the contents together. Use a regular spoon if necessary to mix thoroughly.

2. Next, add a few ice cubes. Pour approximately 4–6 ounces of beer slowly over the ice.

3. Give the cocktail one final stir. Garnish with a mint sprig.

Skip and Go Naked

Serving size = (1) 8–10 ounce cocktail served in a rocks glass.

Drinking a few of thess might inspire you to skip and go naked.

Ingredients:

6–8 ounces light to medium beer (lagers or light ales work nicely)
2 lemon wedges
1 teaspoon powdered sugar
1 ounce of your favorite vodka

Directions:

1. Pour a few ounces of beer, squeeze both lemon wedges, and add sugar. Using a muddler (or end of a large wooden spoon) smash and mix the contents together.

2. Next, add a few ice cubes. Pour the vodka and approximately 4–6 ounces of beer slowly over the ice.

3. Give the cocktail one final stir. Garnish with lemon wedge.

CHAPTER 10

IMPRESS YOUR PALATE—INFUSE FLAVOR USING A COFFEE PRESS

"Beer: So much more than just a breakfast drink."
—Homer Simpson

I originally got this idea when I visited one of my favorite Dayton, Ohio area brewpubs, Lock 27, located in Centerville. For an extra dollar, they have the option to infuse coffee, peppers, or hops in one of their draft beers. I took their idea and added a few of my own. If you don't have a coffee press, for twenty bucks it is a great addition to any bar. Plus it makes a darn good cup of Joe. Once you start pressing fresh ingredients into beer, your Happy Hour will never be the same. The flavors infused by this method are amazing and a cheap way to impress your friends!

Directions:

1. Fill the coffee press with your desired beer.

2. Wait a few minutes for the head to settle.

3. Put infusing ingredients into coffee press and slowly press handle down to infuse beer.

4. Once the press reaches the bottom, wait 3–5 minutes, then slowly pour into a pint glass.

Note: When using hot peppers, be careful not to leave beer in the press very long or you may end up with a super spicy beer that is possibly undrinkable.

Hopped up IPA

Use ½ ounce of your favorite whole hops. I like to use this when I want to really hop up an IPA. But this works well with a pale ale or even a lighter beer. If you like IPAs but don't want the extra calories, you can use this to hop up a low calorie light beer.

Coffee Stout

Use ½ ounce of whole coffee beans. This works best with dark beers like porters and stouts. But don't be shy about using lighter beers like a wheat or light ale.

Pepper Spray

Use a ghost pepper sliced in half. Add to your favorite pale ale, IPA, or even a porter.

Mint Julep

Use ½ ounce of Northern Brewer whole hops and 3–5 fresh mint leaves. A light pale ale works great with this mint flavor. The Northern Brewer hops have a slight minty flavor that pairs nicely with the fresh mint leaves.

Piney for Xmas

Use 1–3 sprigs of fresh rosemary and a small cinnamon stick. Darker stouts and porters taste great with this mix. The Grampa Grimm's Christmas Ale is a real winner with these flavors.

Alternate Version: Vanilla Beanie

Use 1 vanilla bean sliced open to expose the beans. I love this with a nice dark porter or stout. The Grampa Grimm's Christmas Ale tastes great with an extra infusion of vanilla.

CHAPTER 11

BEYOND BLACK & TAN— THE ULTIMATE GUIDE TO LAYERING BEERS

"Whoever drinks beer, he is quick to sleep; whoever sleeps long, does not sin; whoever does not sin, enters Heaven! Thus, let us drink beer!"
—Martin Luther

You never forget your first, and mine was a classic Black & Tan. Since then I have combined almost every dark and light beer that has passed across my bar. From a red eye to the majestic Queens Velvet, the combinations are endless. In my travels I have tried a few that have, to put it lightly, not turned out well. But through painstaking trial and error, below are my winners. If you have any new ideas that rocked your Happy Hour send me a tweet or email so I can try it for myself.

The key to layering beer successfully is to have the correct tool and to use beers with different weights. The lighter, less dense beer needs to go on the top. No matter what color it is. Guinness is served as a nitro-infused beer, so it is fairly light. Layering it on top of most beers will work out great. Some dark beers are dense and heavy and will not work well over a lighter brew. The key is to test a bunch of different combinations or use the list below.

The correct tool is important. In the past I have used a bent spoon to help disperse the top layer of beer when layering. Recently I started using a wonderful tool appropriately named "The Perfect Black and Tan." This tool works great to avoid combining the top layer. It helps to disperse the weight of the top layer and makes the split visible. Feel free to experiment with layering. If you pour two beers together and one sinks to the bottom, try pouring them in reverse.

Directions:

1. Pour the heavier of the two beers to fill a pint glass halfway.

2. Wait for the foam to settle.

3. Using a spoon or other tool, slowly pour lighter beer over top.

4. Admire the cool split between the beers for one minute. Enjoy!

BEER MAKES EVERYTHING BETTER

Combinations I suggest:

1. The Classic Black and Tan—Guinness layered over Bass Ale

2. Black and Blue—Guinness layered over Blue Moon

3. Snakebite—Guinness layered over Hard Cider

4. Black Dog—Guinness (or other stout) layered over Dogfish 60

5. Summer Shandy—Light beer with lemonade. For non-beer drinkers, this could be a gateway beverage.

6. Red Eye—Tomato juice layered over light beer, raw egg dropped in (optional)

7. Queens Velvet—Vanilla Porter layered over Bourbon Barrel Ale

8. Priest collar—Guinness layered over Pear Cider

9. Rattle Snake—Guinness (or other stout) layered over Mexican lager

10. Honey Pack—Packard Porter layered over a Honey Wheat Ale

11. Husky Hipster—Guinness/PBR

SAFETY FIRST

When dropping the shot glass into the beer, the higher you drop it, the more it will splash. That is why you should start with a bar towel under the glass. Also, make sure to cover your teeth with your lips when drinking. The shot glass could slide down and crack you in the teeth. And no one wants a cracked tooth.

CHAPTER 12

BOTTOMS UP— BEER/SHOT COMBOS

"The mouth of a perfectly happy man is filled with beer."
—Egyptian Proverb

If you love beer and also like booze, why not combine the two into one delicious drink sensation? Sometimes people drink shots and chase it with a beer but I say cut out the middleman and put shots directly in your beer! From Classic Boilermakers to never before seen originals like the Going Berserk and Liquid Gold, this chapter will really get your Happy Hour party started, quickly . . . right?

Due to the "spilly" nature of these shots you will need a bar towel to clean up the bar and possibly your face.

Irish Car Bomb

This was the first beer shot I had back when I tended bar at the North Dayton Outback. Like my friend Dave would say, "car bomb coming at ya."

1 dark beer (stouts work best but a nice smooth porter like the Packard Porter on page 120 will do the job)
¾ ounce Irish Whiskey
¾ ounce Baileys or other Irish cream liqueur

Directions:

1. Place a pint (16 ounce) glass on the towel and fill halfway with the beer. Fill a shot glass with half Whiskey, the other half Baileys.

2. To bomb: very carefully (or not) drop the shot glass into the pint glass.

3. Chug quickly! Ingredients will curdle if you don't down it fast. Use the bar towel to clean up anything spilled on the bar or your face.

Note:
This is a great drink to race and see who can finish first.

PRO TIP

If you like American Whiskey, sub the Irish Whiskey for Jack Daniels and call it an "Irish Car Jack."

Flaming Dr. Pepper

I am always surprised how much this shot actually tastes like Dr. Pepper.

1 light beer
1 ounce amaretto
½ ounce 151 Rum or other rum (you will need 151 if you plan on making it "flaming")

Directions:

1. Fill a pint (16 ounce) glass halfway with beer.

2. Fill a shot glass with Amaretto first and top off with 151 rum.

3. Using a lighter very carefully light the shot glass (optional and not recommended).*

4. To bomb: very carefully drop the shot glass into the pint glass.

5. Drink quickly.

6. Use the bar towel to clean up anything spilled on the bar or your face.

*Fire Safety:

I do not recommend lighting the shot on fire and in most states it is illegal to light a drink on fire at a bar. If you do want to light the shot please follow these safety steps:

1. Have a fire extinguisher or other device for putting out a fire close by.

2. Keep your face, hand, hair, towel, and all other body parts and clothing away from the flame.

3. Make sure the fire is out before drinking.

Classic Boilermaker

1 medium to light beer (any
American beer will work)
1½ ounces Whiskey

Directions:

1. Fill a pint (16 ounce) glass halfway with beer. Fill a shot glass with whiskey.

2. To bomb: drop the shot glass into the pint glass.

3. Chug quickly!

4. Use the bar towel to clean up anything spilled on the bar or your face.

Orchard Apple Bomb

1 hard cider (choose your
favorite brand)
1½ ounces cinnamon
whiskey

Directions:

1. Fill a pint (16 ounce) glass halfway with cider.

2. Fill a shot glass with cinnamon whiskey.

3. Drop the shot glass into the pint glass.

4. Chug quickly!

PRO TIP

This makes a nice fall drink.

Jager Bomber

1 can of energy drink
   (choose your favorite
   brand)
1½ ounces Jagermeister

Directions:

1. Fill a pint (16 ounce) glass halfway with energy drink. Fill a shot glass with Jagermeister.

2. To bomb: drop the shot glass into the pint glass.

3. Chug quickly!

4. Use the bar towel to clean up anything spilled on the bar or your face.

PRO TIP

Since this drink is mostly made of an energy drink with lots of caffeine, if you are sensitive to caffeine or are close to calling it a night, this drink is not for you.

Baby Beer Shot

This shot does not have any beer in it but still tastes great. Named after our late friend Ryan who once drank small 7-ounce beers at a party and was known as "Baby Beer" from then on.

Ingredients:
1¼ ounces of Licor 43
¼ ounce half and half

Directions:

1. Fill shot glass most of the way full with the Licor 43.

2. Top off with the half and half.

3. Drink.

Cinnamon Toast Shot

This recipe is dedicated to our friend Troy, who introduced us to this mix while on vacation in Florida.

Ingredients:
¾ ounce cinnamon whiskey (Fireball works great)
¾ ounce of Rumchata liqueur

Directions:

1. Fill shot glass halfway full with cinnamon whiskey and the other half with Rumchata.

2. Drink.

PRO TIP

You can fill a pint glass halfway with a stout or porter and drop the above shot into the glass. Either way it is a tasty drink!

Red White and Blue Balls

A shot inspired by the greatest country in the world. God Bless America!

Ingredients:

1 Pabst Blue Ribbon beer
(bottle or can; either is
fine)
¼ ounce grenadine
½ ounce vodka
½ ounce Blue Curaçao

Directions:

1. Fill a pint glass halfway with PBR.

2. Using a spoon, layer the liquor in a shot glass in the following order:

- Grenadine on the bottom
- Vodka in the middle
- Blue Curaçao on the top

3. To bomb: drop the shot glass into the pint glass.

4. Chug quickly.

5. Place your right hand over your heart and recite the star spangled banner.

PRO TIP

Pabst Blue Ribbon beer is made in America and owned by Americans. It does not get any more patriotic than this drink!

Liquid Gold

Ingredients:

1 regular lager beer (choose
you favorite brand)

1½ ounces Goldschlager

Directions:

1. Fill a pint glass halfway with beer.

2. Fill a shot glass with Goldschlager.

3. Drop the shot glass into the pint glass.

4. Chug quickly!

5. Smile and see if there is any gold stuck in your teeth.

Christmas Fairy Bomb

This shot is perfect for your holiday themed parties.

Ingredients:

1 Festive Christmas beer
(choose your favorite
brand)

¾ ounce cinnamon liqueur

¾ ounce Irish Cream liqueur

Directions:

1. Fill a pint (16 ounce) glass halfway with beer.

2. Fill a shot glass with half cinnamon liqueur and half Irish Cream liqueur.

3. Drop the shot glass into the pint glass.

4. Chug quickly!

PRO TIP

This is a good drink to give Santa when he stops by to deliver packages on Christmas Eve.

BEER MAKES EVERYTHING BETTER

The Most Interesting Shot in the World

Ingredients:
1 Mexican lager (I drink Dos Equis)
1¼ ounce premium tequila
¼ ounce fresh lime juice

Directions:

1. Fill a pint (16 ounce) glass halfway with beer.

2. Fill a shot glass with tequila and top with lime juice.

3. Drop the shot glass into the pint glass.

4. Chug quickly!

PRO TIP

I don't always drink beer shots, but when I do, I drink this one.

Orange Crush

Ingredients:
1 Summer Wheat beer (choose your favorite brand)
¾ ounce orange liqueur
¾ ounce orange vodka

Directions:

1. Fill a pint (16 ounce) glass halfway with beer.

2. Fill a shot glass with half orange liqueur and half orange vodka.

3. Drop the shot glass into the pint glass.

4. Chug quickly.

Going Berserk

Inspired by the Vikings who first brewed beer thousands of years ago.

Ingredients:

1 medium ale
1 hard cider
¾ ounce vodka
¾ ounce hazelnut liqueur

Directions:

1. Fill a pint glass halfway with half ale and half cider.

2. Fill a shot glass with half vodka and half hazelnut liqueur.

3. Drop the shot glass into the pint glass.

4. Chug quickly!

PRO TIP

Drink from a bull horn to feel like a real Viking.

CHAPTER 13

MAKING YOUR OWN BEER

"We brewers don't make beer, we just get all the ingredients together and the beer makes itself."
—Fritz Maytag, President of Anchor Brewing

I will show you ten super easy brewing recipes that will get you started quickly and for minimal investment. The first two recipes will be for making a small one-gallon batch and the rest will be once you upgrade to five-gallon batches. The one-gallon batch is the best way to start and easiest on the wallet. I have included two classic recipes and the rest are John Lemmon original brews you will find only in this book. Each recipe is tried and true with easy to follow directions. Just think, in a few short weeks you will be wowing your friends with your own finished brew. Imagine serving beers you made yourself for your next Happy Hour at home!

David's First IPA 1-gallon recipe

This recipe is named for my oldest brother David, who gave me the idea to start brewing my own beer. Without him I would have never started on this amazing journey.

Ingredients:

1.5 gallons water
2 pounds of Muntons 2-row malted barley
0.25 pounds of Crisp Crystal 15L malted barley
Grain bag
1.5 pounds of Liquid Malt Extract
1-ounce package of Amarillo Hop Pellets, to be used in steps 3–6
Yeast: Safale US–05 dry yeast (half packet)

Bottling

1 ounce of corn sugar (for priming)
10–12 beer bottles with caps

Directions:

1. In a large pot, begin to heat 1.5 gallons of water (spring or good-tasting tap water). Place the crushed malts in a grain bag and tie off the end. Once the water reaches 155°F, turn off the heat and add the grain bag. "Mash" the grain bag for 20 minutes at 150–155°F, stirring occasionally. After 20 minutes remove the grain bag and hold above the pot to let it drain (do not squeeze the bag). The colored water is now called wort.

2. Turn heat on and bring to a boil. Once boiling, remove from heat and slowly mix in the Liquid Malt Extract (LME). Turn heat back on and return to a boil when the LME is thoroughly mixed in.

3. Start 60 minute timer and add (stir in) the bittering hops, .25 ounces Amarillo Pellets.

4. After 30 minutes add the flavoring hops, .25 ounces Amarillo Pellets.

5. After 15 minutes add more flavoring hops, .25 ounces Amarillo Pellets.

6. In 15 more minutes turn off heat and add the final .25 ounces Amarillo Pellets for aroma. Stir wort for a few minutes.

7. Fill a sink with cold water and ice, then put the covered kettle in the ice bath. The goal is to cool the wort to approximately 70–72°F, when the kettle is cool to the touch. The yeast is happiest at these temperatures.

8. Use sanitized hydrometer to measure the O.G. (original gravity).

9. Transfer cooled wort to sanitize fermenting container. Close lid and aerate (slosh back and forth) for 1 minute. Yeast cells need some oxygen for a healthy fermentation.

10. Open fermenter and using sanitized yeast packet and scissors, pour half the packet into the wort.

11. Close lid and install air lock (fill halfway with sanitizer or water).

12. Move fermenter to a cool dark area with an ideal temperature between 65°F and 72°F.

13. After fermentation is complete in 14–21 days your beer will be ready to bottle.

Bottling directions:

1. Clean and sanitize the large pot you used for cooking the beer, the auto-siphon, tubing, bottle filler, and 12 bottles and caps.

2. In a small pot, combine 1 cup of water and 1 ounce of corn sugar. Heat and boil for 5 minutes. Let cool and add to large pot.

3. Open the fermenter. Use the auto-siphon and tubing to transfer the beer into the large pot.

4. Stir slowly to combine the sugar water.

5. Use the auto-siphon and bottle filler to start filling the beer bottles. Make sure you don't overfill the bottles, leaving an inch or so of space at the top of each.

6. Use the capper to cap all the bottles. Place them in a dark area at room temperature.

7. Congratulations! You you have just brewed and bottled your first beer. It normally takes 2 weeks for your beer to be ready to drink. But feel free to wait longer. Your beer will only get better with age.

8. Chill your beer and open and pour into a pint glass. Stare at it for a few minutes and enjoy!

Amber's Easy Ale

This is an easy amber colored ale that is simple but tastes great.

1 Gallon version 1.5 Gallon boil

Ingredients:

Mash (pre-boil tea)
1.5 gallons water
0.25 pounds Cara/pils
0.25 pounds Red wheat
Grain bag

Boil
1.5 pounds Liquid Malt Extract
   (add at the beginning of the
   60 minute boil)
.10 ounces Centennial Hop
   Pellets (bittering) 60 min boil
.10 ounces Centennial Hop
   Pellets (flavoring) 30 min boil
.10 ounces Cascade Hop Pellets
   (flavoring) 15 min boil
.10 ounces Cascade Hop Pellets
   (aroma) 0 min boil (flame out)
Fermentation
Yeast: Safale US-05 dry yeast
   (half packet)

Bottling
1 ounce of corn sugar (for
   priming)
10–12 beer bottles with caps

Target Readings:

Original Gravity	1.054
Final Gravity	1.013
ABV	5.38%
IBU	30

Batch makes 10–12 bottles of beer.

Directions:

1. In a large pot begin to heat 1.5 gallons of water (spring or good-tasting tap water). Place the crushed malts in a grain bag and tie off the end. Once the water reaches 155°F turn off the heat and add the grain bag. "Mash" the grain bag for 20 minutes at 150–155°F, stirring occasionally. After 30 minutes remove the grain bag and hold above the pot to let it drain (do not squeeze the bag). The colored water is now called wort.

2. Turn heat on and bring to a boil. Once boiling, remove from heat and slowly mix in the Liquid Malt Extract (LME). Turn heat back on and return to a boil when the LME is thoroughly mixed in.

3. Start 60 minute timer and add (stir in) the bittering hops, .10 ounces Centennial Pellets.

4. After 30 minutes add the flavoring hops, .10 ounces Centennial Pellets.

5. After 15 minutes add more flavoring hops, .10 ounces Cascade Pellets.

6. In 15 more minutes turn off heat and add the final .10 ounces Cascade Pellets for aroma. Stir wort for a few minutes.

7. Fill a sink with cold water and ice, then put the covered kettle in the ice bath. The goal is to cool the wort to approximately 70–72°F when the kettle is cool to the touch. The yeast is happiest at these temperatures.

8. Transfer cooled wort to sanitized fermenting container. Close lid and aerate (slosh back and forth) for 1 minute. Yeast cells need some oxygen for a healthy fermentation.

9. Open fermenter and using sanitized yeast packet and scissors, pour half the packet into the wort.

10. Use sanitized hydrometer to measure the O.G. (original gravity).

11. Close lid and install air lock (fill halfway with sanitizer or water).

12. Move fermenter to a cool dark area with an idea temperature between 65° and 72°F.

13. After fermentation is complete in 14–21 days your beer will be ready to bottle. Use the bottling directions on page 117.

Packard Porter

This beer is named after the Grimm car dealership that sold Packard's during the 1940s. A solid, smooth bodied Porter reminiscent of the clipper styling of a 1947 Packard.

5 Gallon version 2.5 Gallon boil

Ingredients:
Mash (pre-boil tea)
2.5 gallons water
1 pound Crystal 45L
0.5 pounds Roasted Barley
.75 pounds Pale Chocolate malt
1 pound Cara Brown Malt
Grain bag

Boil
7 pounds Liquid Malt Extract (add at the beginning of the 60 minute boil)
1 ounce Northern Brewer Hop Pellets (bittering) 60 min boil
.50 ounces UK Fuggle Hop Pellets (flavoring) 15 min boil
.50 ounces UK Fuggle Hop Pellets (aroma) 0 min boil (flame out)

Target Readings:

Original Gravity	1.054
Final Gravity	1.014
ABV	5.25%
IBU	35

Batch makes 48–52 bottles of beer.

Directions:

1. In a large pot begin to heat 2.5 gallons of water (spring or good-tasting tap water). Place the crushed malts in a grain bag and tie off the end. Once the water reaches 155°F turn off the heat and add the grain bag. "Mash" the grain bag for 20 minutes at 150–155°F, stirring occasionally. After 20 minutes remove the grain bag and hold above the pot to let it drain (do not squeeze the bag). The colored water is now called wort.

2. Turn heat on and bring to a boil. Once boiling, remove from heat and slowly mix in the Liquid Malt Extract (LME). Turn heat back on and return to a boil when the LME is thoroughly mixed in.

Ingredients:

Fermentation
Yeast: Denny's Favorite 50
 #1450

Bottling
¾ cup of corn sugar
 (for priming)
48–52 beer bottles with caps

Note: Make sure to read and use instructions on yeast packet and "smack" the packet before starting your brew day to give the yeast enough time to get started. This way they will be all ready to pitch with when you are finished brewing.

3. Start 60 minute timer and add (stir in) the bittering hops, 1 ounce Northern Brewer Pellets.

4. After 45 minutes add more flavoring hops, .50 ounces UK Fuggle Pellets.

5. In 15 more minutes turn off heat and add the final .50 ounces UK Fuggle Pellets for aroma. Stir wort for a few minutes.

6. Fill a sink with cold water and ice, then put the covered kettle in the ice bath. The goal is to cool the wort to approximately 70–72°F when the kettle is cool to the touch. The yeast is happiest at these temperatures.

7. Transfer cooled wort to sanitized fermenting container. Add enough clean water to fill container to 5 gallons total. Close lid and aerate (slosh back and forth) for 1 minute. Yeast cells need some oxygen for a healthy fermentation.

8. Open fermenter and using sanitized yeast packet and scissors, pour packet into the wort.

9. Use sanitized hydrometer to measure the O.G. (original gravity).

10. Close lid and install air lock (fill halfway with sanitizer or water).

11. Move fermenter to a cool dark area with an idea temperature between 65°F and 72°F.

12. After fermentation is complete in 14–21 days your beer will be ready to bottle. Use the bottling directions on page 117.

Cascading Centennial Blonde

A light and crisp, easy-drinking blonde with a nice hoppy nose.

5 Gallon version 2.5 Gallon boil

Ingredients:

Mash (pre-boil tea)
2.5 gallons water
1 pound Cara/Pils Malt
Grain bag

Boil
5 pounds Liquid Malt Extract
  (add at the beginning of the
  60 minute boil)
.25 ounces Centennial Hop
  Pellets (bittering) 60 min boil
.25 ounces Centennial Hop
  Pellets (flavoring) 30 min boil
.25 ounces Cascade Hop Pellets
  (flavoring) 15 min boil
.25 ounces Cascade Hop Pellets
  (aroma) 0 min boil (flame out)

Fermentation
Yeast: Safale US-05 dry yeast

Bottling
¾ cup of corn sugar (for priming)
48–52 beer bottles with caps

Target Readings:

Original Gravity	1.040
Final Gravity	1.008
ABV	4.2%
IBU	21

Batch makes 48–52 bottles of beer.

Directions:

1. In a large pot begin to heat 2.5 gallons of water (spring or good-tasting tap water). Place the crushed malts in a grain bag and tie off the end. Once the water reaches 155°F turn off the heat and add the grain bag. "Mash" the grain bag for 20 minutes at 150–155°F, stirring occasionally. After 20 minutes remove the grain bag and hold above the pot to let it drain (do not squeeze the bag). The colored water is now called wort.

2. Turn heat on and bring to a boil. Once boiling, remove from heat and slowly mix in the Liquid Malt Extract (LME). Turn heat back on and return to a boil when the LME is thoroughly mixed in.

3. Start 60 minute timer and add (stir in) the bittering hops, .25 ounces Centennial Pellets.

4. After 15 minutes add more flavoring hops, .25 ounces Centennial Pellets.

5. After 15 minutes add more flavoring hops, .25 ounces Cascade Pellets.

6. In 15 more minutes turn off heat and add the final .25 ounces Cascade Pellets for aroma. Stir wort for a few minutes.

7. Fill a sink with cold water and ice, then put the covered kettle in the ice bath. The goal is to cool the wort to approximately 70–72°F when the kettle is cool to the touch. The yeast is happiest at these temperatures.

8. Transfer cooled wort to sanitized fermenting container. Add enough clean water to fill container to 5 gallons total.

Close lid and aerate (slosh back and forth) for 1 minute. Yeast cells need some oxygen for a healthy fermentation.

9. Open fermenter and using sanitized yeast packet and scissors, pour packet into the wort.

10. Use sanitized hydrometer to measure the O.G. (original gravity).

11. Close lid and install air lock (fill halfway with sanitizer or water).

12. Move fermenter to a cool dark area with an idea temperature between 65°F and 72°F.

13. Pour yourself a well-deserved beer!

14. After fermentation is complete in 14–21 days your beer will be ready to bottle. Use the bottling directions on page 117.

Honey Wheat Ale

This is a mild wheat beer with notes of honey.

5 Gallon version 2.5 Gallon boil

Ingredients:
Mash (pre-boil tea)
2.5 gallons water
2 pounds Red Wheat Malt
1 pound Honey Malt
Grain bag

Boil
7 pounds Liquid Malt Extract
   (add at the beginning of
   the 60 minute boil)
.65 ounces Hallertauer Hop
   Pellets (bittering) 60 min
   boil
.60 ounces Willamette Hop
   Pellets (flavoring) 30 min
   boil

Fermentation
Yeast: Safale US-04 dry yeast

Bottling
¾ cup of corn sugar (for
   priming)
48–52 beer bottles with caps

Target Readings:

Original Gravity	1.050
Final Gravity	1.009
ABV	5.25%
IBU	20

Batch makes 48–52 bottles of beer.

Directions:

1. In a large pot begin to heat 2.5 gallons of water (spring or good-tasting tap water). Place the crushed malts in a grain bag and tie off the end. Once the water reaches 155°F turn off the heat and add the grain bag. "Mash" the grain bag for 20 minutes at 150–155°F, stirring occasionally. After 20 minutes remove the grain bag and hold above the pot to let it drain (do not squeeze the bag). The colored water is now called wort.

2. Turn heat on and bring to a boil. Once boiling, remove from heat and slowly mix in the Liquid Malt Extract (LME). Turn heat back on and return to a boil when the LME is thoroughly mixed in.

3. Start 60 minute timer and add (stir in) the bittering hops, .65 ounces Hallertauer Pellets.

4. After 30 minutes add flavoring hops, .60 ounces Willamette Pellets.

5. In 30 more minutes turn off heat

6. Fill a sink with cold water and ice, then put the covered kettle in the ice bath. The goal is to cool the wort to approximately 70–72°F when the kettle is cool to the touch. The yeast is happiest at these temperatures.

7. Transfer cooled wort to sanitized fermenting container. Add enough clean water to fill container to 5 gallons total. Close lid and aerate (slosh back and forth) for 1 minute. Yeast

cells need some oxygen for a healthy fermentation.

8. Open fermenter and using sanitized yeast packet and scissors, pour packet into the wort.

9. Use sanitized hydrometer to measure the O.G. (original gravity).

10. Close lid and install air lock (fill halfway with sanitizer or water).

11. Move fermenter to a cool dark area with an idea temperature between 65°F and 72°F.

12. After fermentation is complete in 14–21 days your beer will be ready to bottle. Use the bottling directions on page 117.

Yardberry IPA

I bet you are wondering where the idea came from to use yardberries in my beer.

One summer I noticed small wild strawberries growing in my back yard. I picked a few and posted the picture on Facebook. My friend Robb commented "You should put those berries in your next brew". I jokingly told my wife about this and she said "You can't put… yardberries in your beer." I thought, *What a great name*! And the rest is history. This Amercan IPA is my most popular recipe.

5 Gallon version 2.5 Gallon boil

Ingredients:

Mash (pre-boil tea)
2.5 gallons water
1 pound Crystal 45 Malt
½ pounds Cara/pils Malt
Grain bag

Boil
4 pounds Liquid Malt Extract (add at the beginning of the 60 minute boil)
3 pounds Light Dry Malt Extract
.50 ounces Cascade Hop Pellets (bittering) 60 min boil

Target Readings:

Original Gravity	1.056
Final Gravity	1.010
ABV	6.03%
IBU	41

Batch makes 48–52 bottles of beer.

Directions:

1. In a large pot begin to heat 2.5 gallons of water (spring or good-tasting tap water). Place the crushed malts in a grain bag and tie off the end. Once the water reaches 155°F turn off the heat and add the grain bag. "Mash" the grain bag for 20 minutes at 150–155°F, stirring occasionally. After 20 minutes remove the grain bag and hold above the pot to let it drain (do not squeeze the bag). The colored water is now called wort.

.50 ounces Cascade Hop Pellets (bittering) 30 min boil
.50 ounces Citra Hop Pellets (flavoring) 20 min boil
4 ounces strawberries, or Yardberries if you can find them! 15 min boil
.50 ounces Hullmelon Hop Pellets (flavoring) 10 min boil
.50 ounces Hullmelon Hop Pellets (flavoring) 5 min boil
.50 ounces Citra Hop Pellets (aroma) 0 min boil
2 ounces Citra Hop Pellets (dry hop) 5–7 days

Fermentation
Yeast: Safale US-05 dry yeast

Bottling
¾ cup of corn sugar (for priming)
48–52 beer bottles with caps

2. Turn heat on and bring to a boil. Once boiling, remove from heat and slowly mix in the Liquid Malt Extract (LME) and Dry Malt Extract (DME). Turn heat back on and return to a boil when the LME and DME are thoroughly mixed in.

3. Start 60 minute timer and add (stir in) the bittering hops, .50 ounces Cascade Hop Pellets.

4. After 30 minutes add flavoring hops, .50 ounces Cascade Pellets.

5. After 10 minutes add flavoring hops, .50 ounces Citra Pellets.

6. After 5 minutes add 4 ounces strawberries.

7. After 5 minutes add flavoring hops, .50 ounces Hullmelon Pellets

8. After 5 minutes add flavoring hops, .50 ounces Hullmelon Pellets

9. In 5 more minutes turn off heat and add the final .50 ounces Citra Pellets for aroma. Stir wort for a few minutes.

10. Fill a sink with cold water and ice, then put the covered kettle in the ice bath. The goal is to cool the wort to approximately 70–72°F when the kettle is cool to the touch. The yeast is happiest at these temperatures.

11. Transfer cooled wort to sanitized fermenting container. Add enough clean water to fill container to 5 gallons total. Close lid and aerate (slosh back and forth) for 1 minute. Yeast cells need some oxygen for a healthy fermentation.

12. Open fermenter and using sanitized yeast packet and scissors, pour the packet into the wort.

13. Use sanitized hydrometer to measure the O.G. (original gravity).

14. Close lid and install air lock (fill halfway with sanitizer or water).

15. Move fermenter to a cool dark area with an idea temperature between 65°F and 72°F.

16. After the main fermentation is complete, normally 10–14 days, add 2 ounces of Citra pellets to the fermenter for 5–7 days. This method is called dry hopping and will give your final beer a great aroma.

After fermentation is complete in 14–21 days, your beer will be ready to bottle. Use the bottling directions on page 117.

Gold Pants Pale Ale

A light golden ale named after the token earned by a certain Ohio football team for beating That Team up North.

5 Gallon version 2.5 Gallon boil

Ingredients:

Mash (pre-boil tea)
2.5 gallons water
.5 pounds Crystal 45 Malt
.25 pounds Crystal 77 Malt
1 pound Cara/pils Malt
Grain bag

Boil
7 pounds Liquid Malt Extract (add at
   the beginning of the 60 minute boil)
.50 ounces Centennial Hop Pellets
   (bittering) 45 min boil
.50 ounces Centennial Hop Pellets
   (bittering) 15 min boil
.50 ounces Amarillo Hop Pellets
   (flavoring) 5 min boil
.50 ounces Amarillo Hop Pellets
   (flavoring) 0 min boil

Fermentation
Yeast: Safale US-05 dry yeast

Bottling
¾ cup of corn sugar (for priming)
48–52 beer bottles with caps

Target Readings:

Original Gravity	1.048
Final Gravity	1.010
ABV	5%
IBU	25

Batch makes 48–52 bottles of beer.

Directions:

1. In a large pot begin to heat 2.5 gallons of water (spring or good-tasting tap water). Place the crushed malts in a grain bag and tie off the end. Once the water reaches 155°F turn off the heat and add the grain bag. "Mash" the grain bag for 20 minutes at 150–155°F, stirring occasionally. After 20 minutes remove the grain bag and hold above the pot to let it drain (do not squeeze the bag). The colored water is now called wort.

2. Turn heat on and bring to a boil. Once boiling, remove from heat and slowly mix in the Liquid Malt Extract (LME). Turn heat

back on and return to a boil when the LME is thoroughly mixed in.

3. Start 60 minute timer and after 15 minutes add (stir in) the bittering hops, .50 ounces Centennial Pellets.

4. After 30 minutes add flavoring hops, .50 ounces Centennial Pellets.

5. After 10 minutes add flavoring hops, .50 ounces Amarillo Pellets.

6. In 5 more minutes turn off heat and add the final .50 ounces Amarillo Pellets for aroma. Stir wort for a few minutes.

7. Fill a sink with cold water and ice, then put the covered kettle in the ice bath. The goal is to cool the wort to approximately 70–72°F when the kettle is cool to the touch. The yeast is happiest at these temperatures.

8. Transfer cooled wort to sanitized fermenting container. Add enough clean water to fill container to 5 gallons total. Close lid and aerate (slosh back and forth) for 1 minute. Yeast cells need some oxygen for a healthy fermentation.

9. Open fermenter and using sanitized yeast packet and scissors, pour packet into the wort.

10. Use sanitized hydrometer to measure the O.G. (original gravity).

11. Close lid and install air lock (fill halfway with sanitizer or water).

12. Move fermenter to a cool dark area with an idea temperature between 65°F and 72°F.

13. Pour yourself a well-deserved beer!

14. After fermentation is complete in 14–21 days your beer will be ready to bottle. Use the bottling directions on page 117.

The Jessica Red

I named this beer after my wonderful wife, Jessica.

A complex slightly sweet red ale with notes of chocolate telling a compelling story.

5 Gallon version 2.5 Gallon boil

Ingredients:
Mash (pre-boil tea)
2.5 gallons water
1 pound Light Munich
.5 pounds Caramunich
.5 pounds Special B Malt
.02 pounds Chocolate Malt
Grain bag

Boil
7 pounds Liquid Malt Extract
   (add at the beginning of the 60
   minute boil)
.44 ounces Northern Brewer Hop
   Pellets (bittering) 60 min boil
.28 ounces Northern Brewer Hop
   Pellets (flavoring) 20 min boil

Fermentation
Yeast: Safale US-05 dry yeast

Bottling
¾ cup of corn sugar (for priming)
48–52 beer bottles with caps

Target Readings:

Original Gravity	1.054
Final Gravity	1.012
ABV	5.51%
IBU	20

Batch makes 48–52 bottles of beer.

Directions:

1. In a large pot begin to heat 2.5 gallons of water (spring or good tasting tap water). Place the crushed malts in a grain bag and tie off the end. Once the water reaches 155°F turn off the heat and add the grain bag. "Mash" the grain bag for 20 minutes at 150–155°F, stirring occasionally. After 20 minutes remove the grain bag and hold above the pot to let it drain (do not squeeze the bag). The colored water is now called wort.

2. Turn heat on and bring to a boil. Once boiling, remove from heat and slowly mix in the Liquid Malt Extract

(LME). Turn heat back on and return to a boil when the LME is thoroughly mixed in.

3. Start 60 minute timer and add (stir in) the bittering hops, .44 ounces Northern Brewer Pellets.

4. After 40 minutes add flavoring hops, .28 ounces Northern Brewer Pellets.

5. After 20 more minutes turn off heat.

6. Fill a sink with cold water and ice, then put the covered kettle in the ice bath. The goal is to cool the wort to approximately 70–72°F when the kettle is cool to the touch. The yeast is happiest at these temperatures.

7. Transfer cooled wort to sanitized fermenting container. Add enough clean water to fill container to 5 gallons total. Close lid and aerate (slosh back and forth)

for 1 minute. Yeast cells need some oxygen for a healthy fermentation.

8. Open fermenter and using sanitized yeast packet and scissors, pour packet into the wort.

9. Use sanitized hydrometer to measure the O.G. (original gravity).

10. Close lid and install air lock (fill halfway with sanitizer or water).

11. Move fermenter to a cool dark area with an idea temperature between 65°F and 72°F.

12. Pour yourself a well-deserved beer!

13. After fermentation is complete in 14–21 days your beer will be ready to bottle. Use the bottling directions on page 117.

BEER MAKES EVERYTHING BETTER

In A Galaxy IPA

This beer comes from a galaxy far, far away . . .

5 Gallon version 2.5 Gallon boil

Ingredients:

Mash (pre-boil tea)
2.5 gallons water
2 pounds 2 Row malt
1 pound Flaked Wheat
1 pound Cara Amber
.5 pounds Crystal 77 Malt
.25 pounds Crystal 77 Malt
1 pound Cara/pils Malt
Grain bag

Boil
7 pounds Liquid Malt
  Extract (add at the
  beginning of the 60
  minute boil)
.50 ounces Centennial Hop
  Pellets (bittering) 60 min
  boil
.50 ounces Centennial Hop
  Pellets (bittering) 30 min
  boil
.50 ounces Galaxy Hop
  Pellets (flavoring) 15 min
  boil

Target Readings:

Original Gravity	1.061
Final Gravity	1.011
ABV	6.56%
IBU	60

Batch makes 48–52 bottles of beer.

Directions:

1. In a large pot begin to heat 2.5 gallons of water (spring or good tasting tap water). Place the crushed malts in a grain bag and tie off the end. Once the water reaches 155°F turn off the heat and add the grain bag. "Mash" the grain bag for 20 minutes at 150–155°F, stirring occasionally. After 20 minutes remove the grain bag and hold above the pot to let it drain (do not squeeze the bag). The colored water is now called wort.

2. Turn heat on and bring to a boil. Once boiling, remove from heat and slowly mix in the Liquid Malt Extract (LME). Turn heat back on and return to a boil when the LME is thoroughly mixed in.

3. Start 60 minute timer and add (stir in) the bittering hops, .50 ounces Centennial Pellets.

.50 ounces Galaxy Hop
Pellets (flavoring) 0 min
boil

Fermentation
Yeast: Safale US-05 dry
yeast
1 ounce Galaxy Hop Pellets
(dry hop) after main
fermentation is complete

Bottling
½ cup of corn sugar (for
priming)
48–52 beer bottles with caps

4. After 30 minutes add bittering hops, .50 ounces Centennial Pellets.

5. After 15 minutes add flavoring hops, .50 ounces Galaxy Pellets.

6. In 15 more minutes turn off heat and add the final .50 ounces Galaxy Pellets for aroma. Stir wort for a few minutes.

7. Fill a sink with cold water and ice, then put the covered kettle in the ice bath. The goal is to cool the wort to approximately 70–72°F when the kettle is cool to the touch. The yeast is happiest at these temperatures.

8. Transfer cooled wort to sanitized fermenting container. Add enough clean water to fill container to 5 gallons total. Close lid and aerate (slosh back and forth) for 1 minute. Yeast cells need some oxygen for a healthy fermentation.

9. Open fermenter and using sanitized yeast packet and scissors, pour packet into the wort.

10. Use sanitized hydrometer to measure the O.G. (original gravity).

11. Close lid and install airlock (fill halfway with sanitizer or water).

12. Move fermenter to a cool dark area with an idea temperature between 65°F and 72°F.

13. After 10–14 days the main fermentation will be finished. You will notice that the airlock will go from bubbling almost constantly to very little. At this point, open the fermentation container and pour in the 1 ounce of Galaxy hops. This is called "dry hopping" the beer and will give this brew an extra punch of hop aroma.

14. After fermentation is complete in 14–21 days your beer will be ready to bottle. Use the bottling directions on page 117.

⅛th **Irish Stout**

A classic Irish Stout, dark in color with a nice bitter finish. Kiss me I'm ⅛th Irish.

5 Gallon version 2.5 Gallon boil

Ingredients:
Mash (pre-boil tea)
2.5 gallons water
.5 pounds Roasted Barley
.40 pounds Chocolate Malt
.25 pounds Crystal 77 Malt
Grain bag

Boil
4 pounds Dried Malt Extract (add at the beginning of the 60 minute boil)
.5 pounds Cane Sugar (add at the beginning of the 60 minute boil)
1 ounce Target Hop Pellets (bittering) 60 min boil
.25 ounces EKG (East Kent Golding) Hop Pellets (flavoring) 15 min boil

Fermentation
Yeast: Safale US-04 dry yeast

Bottling
¾ cup of corn sugar (for priming)
48–52 beer bottles with caps

Target Readings:

Original Gravity	1.042
Final Gravity	1.009
ABV	4.2%
IBU	20

Batch makes 48–52 bottles of beer.

Directions:

1. In a large pot begin to heat 2.5 gallons of water (spring or good-tasting tap water). Place the crushed malts in a grain bag and tie off the end. Once the water reaches 155°F turn off the heat and add the grain bag. "Mash" the grain bag for 20 minutes at 150–155°F, stirring occasionally. After 20 minutes remove the grain bag and hold above the pot to let it drain (do not squeeze the bag). The colored water is now called wort.

2. Turn heat on and bring to a boil. Once boiling, remove from heat and slowly mix in the Dried Malt Extract (DME)

and cane sugar. Turn heat back on and return to a boil when the LME is thoroughly mixed in.

3. Start 60 minute timer and add (stir in) the bittering hops 1 ounce Target Pellets.

4. After 45 minutes add flavoring hops .25 ounces EKG (East Kent Golding) Pellets.

5. After 15 more minutes turn off heat.

6. Fill a sink with cold water and ice, then put the covered kettle in the ice bath. The goal is to cool the wort to approximately 70–72°F when the kettle is cool to the touch. The yeast is happiest at these temperatures.

7. Transfer cooled wort to sanitized fermenting container. Add enough clean water to fill container to

5 gallons total. Close lid and aerate (slosh back and forth) for 1 minute. Yeast cells need some oxygen for a healthy fermentation.

8. Open fermenter and using sanitized yeast packet and scissors, pour packet into the wort.

9. Use sanitized hydrometer to measure the O.G. (original gravity).

10. Close lid and install air lock (fill halfway with sanitizer or water).

11. Move fermenter to a cool dark area with an idea temperature between 65°F and 72°F.

12. Pour yourself a well-deserved beer!

13. After fermentation is complete in 14–21 days your beer will be ready to bottle. Use the bottling directions on page 117.

CHAPTER 14

RAISING THE BAR—ON THE CHEAP, SEMI-SERIOUS, OR ALL THE WAY

I have tended bar at numerous restaurants and pubs, drank at many saloons, and even built my own basement bar called The Lemmon Lounge. Setting up your own bar can be as easy as arranging a few tables on your patio or as complex as installing a twelve-tap keg cooler in your garage. I have seen great bar setups in small apartments and elaborate medieval style setups in ten thousand square foot model homes. You can go as big or as small as you like based on your space and funding. This chapter will help you put together the perfect, user-friendly bar for your specific situation.

Below are the seven steps to setting up your bar. These are the same seven components you need no matter what size or type of bar you are making.

1. Determine your space

Do you have a 10 feet by 10 feet patio, a cubby hole in the basement, or half the garage? This is the first step determine your space. The first Lemmon Lounge I made was in the basement of our first apartment and consisted of a couch, a table, and a TV. We added the wall decorations later but used what we had. So start with making a decision on what space you will be using. You do not have to pick a large spot. It will amaze you what can be done with a small space. One bar I used to manage was originally in a small space with lower ceilings and a short bar area. After they upgraded to a much larger "sports bar" area, I remember hearing the regular patrons saying it lost some of the character they loved about the old place. So don't be scared of using a small amount of space. If it looks too small you can use strategically placed mirrors to give it a bigger look. In the end the people really make the bar. Pick your space and move on.

2. Plan your type of beverage dispenser

The type of beverages and how you plan to dispense them will make a big difference in how you use the space you determined in step #1. If you are using a fancy keg draft system you will arrange things differently than if you just iced down a cooler of beer cans. If you are making this a martini bar you will need more space dedicated to bottles, ice shakers, and martini glasses.

I suggest you plan your bar around your beverage dispenser because you will need easy access to the star of the show. Having worked at a few non-user-friendly bars in my day trust me you want to plan this step carefully. Make sure you test how beverages will be poured and make sure you space for more than one person in the pouring/making station at a time. This will keep the line down and the natives will not get restless waiting for their next drink.

3. Stock your beverages

The stars of the show are your beverages, drinks if you will. Make sure you stock up. As a rule you will need more than you think.

I like to think of it this way: too much is never a problem but running out can be a huge one.

Once, back in my Outback bartending days I attended a party that ran out of beer. Normally not an issue—just have someone perform a B, double E, double R, UN beer run, right? Wrong. In Ohio the state bans stores from selling alcohol after 2:30 a.m. and we had run out of time. Since we worked second shift our party had just gotten started. Luckily my friend Matt had a solution. Being the manager he had access to a secret stash: The beer cooler, complete with keys and security clearance, since the owner allowed us to buy beer from the restaurant. So we decided to make a pilgrimage to this untapped resource and pay it back in the morning. Soon we were in and out with a small stash before anyone was the wiser. Our party continued and we paid our tab the next day. My moral to this looong story is, unless you manage a restaurant where you can make a 3:00 a.m. beer run, make sure you stock up.

4. Decorations

Simple is always better. Use what you have before making a purchase. If you are decorating a basement bar, using a framed, flattened six-pack holder of your favorite brew is better than buying neon beer signs. You could even have your friends sign one dollar bills and tape them on the wall. This makes for a homey feel and you can always pull a few down if you are short on cash for a beer run. Don't make it complicated. Two cheap beer signs from a local flea market can go a long way.

5. Seating/standing

Now that you have your bar mostly together, perform a dry run. Walk around the bar and pretend to pour yourself a beverage. Then picture a group of your friends filling the space and see what works. For a bar to be popular it needs to function well and being user friendly can make a big difference. Keep in mind some people like to sit and some like to stand. Make sure you have room for each. The star of the show may be the drinks but good conversation is what makes it truly a great party. Having open seating areas, or standing areas, where your friends can mingle and converse is important. I personally enjoy places where I can talk with multiple people and not have to shout.

6. Check your flow

Make sure there is room for more than one person to use the beverage station at a time. You do not want a backup or long line to mess up your vibe. Before opening, take ten minutes to walk around and sit in each seat. This will help you make adjustments if needed. Picture the size of the group you have invited and design things for a better flow. Test sitting in each seat will alert you to any flaws you may have. Make adjustments as needed. Remember everyone likes to have a good seat.

7. Give it a good name!

Like Cheers, you need to name your bar so people will know where they are and where they can check in to make their friends jealous when posting on social media. The Lemmon Lounge was easy since my last name is Lemmon and the word lounge starts with an L. It has changed location a few times but still maintained its consistency. Giving your bar a great name can be tough but don't overcomplicate it. You can name it after yourself, like George's Garage Dive; your dog, like Bailey's Bistro; your favorite fictional hero, like Shane's Shanti; your great uncle, like Jim's Bar and Grill; or even use a Viking god, like Odin's Horn Hall. (That last one sounded naughty!) If you have namer's block (is that a real thing?), I suggest you go to your bar, pour yourself a beverage, sit down with a pen and paper, and start writing down ideas. If you are still stuck, start with letters of the alphabet. Write down a word for each letter. Angle, Bagel, Cabinet, Doofus . . . Once you have had a few beverages your mind will loosen up and the ideas will start flowing, and I am willing to guess you will have your perfect bar name before you get to Zephyr.

CHAPTER 15

Host Your Own Happy Hour—Show Off What You've Cooked Up

This is one of my favorite chapters because learning how to impress your friends is fun and this book is all about fun. Having people beg to be invited to my next soiree was always my goal.

There are five main basics to throwing a magnificent party. You can raise or lower each level in awesomeness with the amount of effort and money you plan on using.

The five basics of parties are: theme, beverage setup, food, music, and transportation.

Theme

All memorable parties start with a theme or reason for the get-together. This can be simple like a bonfire, football game, or birthday party. More elaborate themes would include Mexican fiesta, redneck BBQ, or superhero costume party. Your theme is only restricted by your imagination. The theme is all about the experience you want your guests to have. One of my most successful parties was a birthday party where I had booked one of my favorite bands. I invited everyone I knew and mentioned the band would be there. It ended up the lead singer was sick and they had to cancel. We hosted the party anyway and everyone had a great time in spite of this setback. Theme is important but don't let it hold you back. If you just want to hang with a few close friends give it a simple theme like Monday Mixer, Spring Spicer or Bring a Beer Cookout.

Beverage setup

Having spent a large amount of my life as a bartender, I believe this step is just as important as Theme. Similar to step #2 from the last chapter, choosing the beverages is paramount. Serving mimosas for an evening bonfire party would be odd. Just like having Double IPAs on the menu for an early morning breakfast test kitchen might raise a few eyebrows. Matching the time of day with the beverage selection plus making sure everything is freshest and at the correct temperature when served is imperative. Think this part through and always get extra ice.

Food

All great parties have a nice food assortment. Matching the food with the theme and beverages increases your odds for success. Once I have the theme in mind I like to start brainstorming food ideas. Make sure you have plenty of food for each guest. Soaking up part of the alcohol is most of its job. This book is filled with great food recipes and all will work well for a party. Flip back through chapter 7 for some inspiration.

Music

If food and beverages are the stars, music is your scheme. This often overlooked element is a requirement in my book. First off, the volume level is just as important as what music is being played. If you are having a quiet intimate party you do not want to be blasting party mix music. Pick music that aligns with your theme. Plan a play list ahead of time if possible. If you only have time to put together a short one have it on repeat in case the party goes longer than planned. You can always use Pandora or some other such app to be your DJ. They have different stations you can use and most are free.

Use music that all your guests will enjoy, not just your faves. I have been to parties where the host asks for short playlists from the crowd to keep things going.

Place the speakers away from the direct path where your guests will be seated or gather. If not, the music will get drowned out by the raised volume they will be making in an attempt to communicate. The volume will increase as the party goes on.

Whatever tunes you decide on, music is an important part of your party!

Transportation

If you are serving alcohol it is your responsibility to ensure every guest has safe transportation home. From designated drivers, to Uber, to calling a cab, to having room for guests to crash for the night. It is your party so take this part seriously. Paying for a friend's cab or Uber ride home is much cheaper than the regret of letting them drive home while impaired. Safety first!

ACKNOWLEDGMENTS

To my agent Nicole, who made this possible. My editors Nicole Frail, Leah Zarra, and all the team at Skyhorse Publishing.

My oldest brother David Lemmon, who studied family history and informed me about our brewing background. My great-great-grandfather Johann Grimm. I never met you, but I am continuing your brewing legacy.

My brother in law and best buddy, Nick Long, for helping me with some photos. You were also a big help with drinking any mistakes.

My design team, Rob and Carol Betts, for their help with my branding and website.

Brian and Justin Koehen, the owners of Star City Brewing for their partnership on the Hippo IPA. Dylan, the bartender, and the rest of our friends at Star City Brewing.

And finally, to my mom and dad, who always encouraged my to follow my dreams and let me know I could be successful.

Index

Wrap
   Cerveza-Battered Halibut Wrap, 34

Y
Yardberry IPA, 126–128
Yeast, 11

Yogurt
   Lager Roasted Turkey Gyro with "T"
     Sauce, 47

Z
Zucchini
   Pasta with White Ale Cream Sauce, 49